INTRODUCING
ISSUES WITH
OPPOSING
VIEWPOINTS®

Garbage and Recycling

Lauri S. Friedman, *Book Editor*

GREENHAVEN PRESS
A part of Gale, Cengage Learning

GALE
CENGAGE Learning™

Detroit • New York • San Francisco • New Haven, Conn • Waterville, Maine • London

363.728
Dav

Christine Nasso, *Publisher*
Elizabeth Des Chenes, *Managing Editor*

© 2009 Greenhaven Press, a part of Gale, Cengage Learning

Gale and Greenhaven Press are registered trademarks used herein under license.

For more information, contact:
Greenhaven Press
27500 Drake Rd.
Farmington Hills, MI 48331-3535
Or you can visit our Internet site at gale.cengage.com

For product information and technology assistance, contact us at

Gale Customer Support, 1-800-877-4253
For permission to use material from this text or product, submit all requests online at
www.cengage.com/permissions

Further permissions questions can be emailed to permissionrequest@cengage.com

Articles in Greenhaven Press anthologies are often edited for length to meet page requirements. In addition, original titles of these works are changed to clearly present the main thesis and to explicitly indicate the author's opinion. Every effort is made to ensure that Greenhaven Press accurately reflects the original intent of the authors. Every effort has been made to trace the owners of copyrighted material.

Cover Image © 2009/Jupiterimages.

LIBRARY OF CONGRESS CATALOGING-IN-PUBLICATION DATA

Garbage and recycling / Lauri S. Friedman, book editor.
    p. cm. — (Introducing issues with opposing viewpoints)
  Includes bibliographical references and index.
  ISBN 978-0-7377-4337-1 (hardcover)
  1. Refuse and refuse disposal—Juvenile literature. 2. Recycling (Waste, etc.)—Juvenile literature. 3. Environmental policy—Juvenile literature. I. Friedman, Lauri S.
  TD792.G367 2009
  363.72'88—dc22

                                                              2008049191

Printed in the United States of America
  2 3 4 5 6 7 13 12 11 10 09

Contents

Foreword

I ndulging in a wide spectrum of ideas, beliefs, and perspectives is a critical cornerstone of democracy. After all, it is often debates over differences of opinion, such as whether to legalize abortion, how to treat prisoners, or when to enact the death penalty, that shape our society and drive it forward. Such diversity of thought is frequently regarded as the hallmark of a healthy and civilized culture. As the Reverend Clifford Schutjer of the First Congregational Church in Mansfield, Ohio, declared in a 2001 sermon, "Surrounding oneself with only like-minded people, restricting what we listen to or read only to what we find agreeable is irresponsible. Refusing to entertain doubts once we make up our minds is a subtle but deadly form of arrogance." With this advice in mind, Introducing Issues with Opposing Viewpoints books aim to open readers' minds to the critically divergent views that comprise our world's most important debates.

Introducing Issues with Opposing Viewpoints simplifies for students the enormous and often overwhelming mass of material now available via print and electronic media. Collected in every volume is an array of opinions that captures the essence of a particular controversy or topic. Introducing Issues with Opposing Viewpoints books embody the spirit of nineteenth-century journalist Charles A. Dana's axiom: "Fight for your opinions, but do not believe that they contain the whole truth, or the only truth." Absorbing such contrasting opinions teaches students to analyze the strength of an argument and compare it to its opposition. From this process readers can inform and strengthen their own opinions, or be exposed to new information that will change their minds. Introducing Issues with Opposing Viewpoints is a mosaic of different voices. The authors are statesmen, pundits, academics, journalists, corporations, and ordinary people who have felt compelled to share their experiences and ideas in a public forum. Their words have been collected from newspapers, journals, books, speeches, interviews, and the Internet, the fastest growing body of opinionated material in the world.

Introducing Issues with Opposing Viewpoints shares many of the well-known features of its critically acclaimed parent series, Opposing Viewpoints. The articles are presented in a pro/con format, allowing readers to absorb divergent perspectives side by side. Active reading questions preface each viewpoint, requiring the student to approach the material thoughtfully and carefully. Useful charts, graphs, and cartoons supplement each article. A thorough introduction provides readers with crucial background on an issue. An annotated bibliography points the reader toward articles, books, and Web sites that contain additional information on the topic. An appendix of organizations to contact contains a wide variety of charities, nonprofit organizations, political groups, and private enterprises that each hold a position on the issue at hand. Finally, a comprehensive index allows readers to locate content quickly and efficiently.

Introducing Issues with Opposing Viewpoints is also significantly different from Opposing Viewpoints. As the series title implies, its presentation will help introduce students to the concept of opposing viewpoints and learn to use this material to aid in critical writing and debate. The series' four-color, accessible format makes the books attractive and inviting to readers of all levels. In addition, each viewpoint has been carefully edited to maximize a reader's understanding of the content. Short but thorough viewpoints capture the essence of an argument. A substantial, thought-provoking essay question placed at the end of each viewpoint asks the student to further investigate the issues raised in the viewpoint, compare and contrast two authors' arguments, or consider how one might go about forming an opinion on the topic at hand. Each viewpoint contains sidebars that include at-a-glance information and handy statistics. A Facts About section located in the back of the book further supplies students with relevant facts and figures.

Following in the tradition of the Opposing Viewpoints series, Greenhaven Press continues to provide readers with invaluable exposure to the controversial issues that shape our world. As John Stuart Mill once wrote: "The only way in which a human being can make some approach to knowing the whole of a subject is by hearing what can be said about it by persons of every variety of opinion and studying all modes in which it can be looked at by every character of mind. No wise man ever acquired his wisdom in any mode but this." It is to this principle that Introducing Issues with Opposing Viewpoints books are dedicated.

Introduction

Anyone who has visited one of America's many beaches has probably seen a piece of garbage get tossed about by the waves or wash up on shore. It is possible that this piece of trash was littered by a careless pedestrian or blown out of a nearby overflowing trash can. But it is also increasingly possible that this piece of garbage originated not from on land but from a gigantic, swirling, island of garbage in the Pacific Ocean that is growing in size, strength, and danger.

For years scientists have been tracking the problematic build-up of garbage in the ocean. According to the United Nations Environment Programme, every square mile of ocean now contains forty-six thousand pieces of floating plastic. In August 1997 Captain Charles Moore stumbled upon a garbage problem that was larger than most people had ever imagined. As he sailed his boat *Alguita* through a patch of Pacific water known as the North Pacific Gyre, he encountered what can only be described as a floating continent of trash. Remembers Moore, "As I gazed from the deck at the surface of what ought to have been a pristine ocean, I was confronted, as far as the eye could see, with the sight of plastic." Moore sailed through the trash soup for more than a week, encountering nothing but waste and debris. "It seemed unbelievable, but I never found a clear spot," said Moore. "In the week it took to cross the subtropical high, no matter what time of day I looked, plastic debris was floating everywhere: bottles, bottle caps, wrappers, fragments."[1]

The entity Moore had stumbled upon has come to be known by several names: "trash vortex," "plastic soup," the "Great Pacific Garbage Patch," and more formally, the "Eastern Garbage Patch." Once estimated to be twice the size of Texas, it is now believed to be double the area of the continental United States. It stretches a huge distance across the ocean, beginning about five hundred miles off the California coast, past Hawaii, and almost as far as Japan. The trash is 80 percent plastic, and there is as much as 100 million tons of it. It cannot be seen from space because the debris sits just below the surface of the water and in some areas extends deep into the water column. For all intents and purposes, it is the world's largest garbage dump and a growing environmental hazard.

A sample of garbage collected by Charles Moore from the North Pacific Gyre in his journey across the Pacific. Moore sailed for weeks through a seemingly endless "continent of trash."

Researchers estimate the garbage patch began to form at some point in the 1950s. The trash is kept in a group by underwater currents that swirl it together, solidifying it as an entity. Indeed, the gyre in which the garbage has collected is home to a circular current that normally rounds up flotsam and jetsam in the sea, allowing microorganisms to biodegrade it. But plastic, which takes hundreds of years to decompose, has proven too durable for this process—thus it continues to accumulate in the gyre, swirling and swirling with no end in sight.

Ian Kiernan, an Australian environmentalist who first saw the trash soup on an around-the-world solo yacht race, was sickened by the diversity of items he saw floating on the open sea. "It was just filled with things like furniture, fridges, plastic containers, cigarette lighters, plastic bottles, light globes, televisions and fishing nets,"[2] he recalled. Incredibly, objects that are half a century old have been found floating in the garbage patch. This is because "every little piece of plastic manufactured in the past 50 years that made it into the ocean is still out there somewhere,"[3] explains chemist Tony Andrady.

While plastic does not biodegrade, it does *photo*degrade—that is, light from the sun breaks pieces of plastic into smaller and smaller bits, not breaking them down but making them smaller. As the plastic chips break apart or leach, they are eaten or absorbed by marine animals, which the UN Environment Programme says kills more than a million seabirds and more than 100,000 marine mammals every year. There are further consequences for the humans who eat these animals when they are fished and brought to market. The chemicals leached by plastic have been linked to cancer and birth defects, and they have been found to attract other toxins such as hydrocarbons and pesticides. "What goes into the ocean goes into these animals and onto your dinner plate," says ocean researcher Marcus Eriksen. "It's that simple."[4] Many doubt the garbage patch is able to be cleaned up—its size and location in the water column would hinder most reasonable cleanup efforts. Worse, scientists have warned citizens of all countries that if humans do not cut their use of plastic or practice efforts to recycle plastic and keep it out of the world's oceans, the garbage patch could double in size over the next ten years.

The Great Pacific Garbage Patch is one example of how humans are beginning to see the effects trash has had on the planet. The impact of trash on the oceans is just one of the many issues explored in *Introducing Issues with Opposing Viewpoints: Garbage and Recycling*. Readers will also consider arguments about whether recycling is cost-effective, whether we are running out of room for garbage, and what role the government should play in guiding Americans' consumption and garbage habits. Readers will examine these questions in the article pairs and form their own opinions on the problem of garbage and the promise of recycling.

Notes

1. Charles Moore, "Across the Pacific Ocean, Plastics, Plastics, Everywhere," *Natural History*, vol. 112, no. 9, November 2003.
2. Quoted in Amanda Woods, "The Plastic Killing Fields," *Sydney Morning Herald* (Sydney, Australia), December 29, 2007.
3. Quoted in Kathy Marks and Daniel Howden, "The World's Rubbish Dump: A Garbage Tip That Stretches from Hawaii to Japan," *Independent* (London), February 5, 2008. www.independent.co.uk/environment/the-worlds-rubbish-dump-a-garbage-tip-that-stretches-from-hawaii-to-japan-778016.html.
4. Quoted in Marks and Howden, "The World's Rubbish Dump."

Chapter 1

Is Garbage a Serious Problem?

Consumer societies like the United States typically buy large quantities of disposable goods, which produce massive amounts of garbage.

We Are Running Out of Room for Garbage

David Lazarus

"The United States is awash in garbage, and we're rapidly running out of ways to dispose of it."

In the following viewpoint David Lazarus argues that Americans generate so much trash, they are running out of places to put it. One reason that Americans make so much garbage is their addiction to disposable goods, he explains. Indeed, Americans typically buy mass quantities of disposable items and constantly purchase new computers, televisions, and CD players rather than buy used items or get products repaired. In Lazarus's opinion, the trash problem is worsened when companies urge people to buy more and more of their products. Despite dozens of landfills and successful recycling programs, Americans generate more trash than they have space in which to dispose of it. Lazarus concludes by offering solutions to the problem, such as converting garbage to energy, recycling it, and stepping up conservation efforts.

Lazarus is a former columnist for the *San Francisco Chronicle*, from which this viewpoint is taken. He now writes regularly for the *Los Angeles Times*.

AS YOU READ, CONSIDER THE FOLLOWING QUESTIONS:
1. How much garbage does each American produce every day, according to the author?
2. What does the word "hyper-consumerism" mean in the context of the viewpoint?
3. According to Lazarus, what percent of trash is being diverted away from landfills in California?

T he garbage now piling up on East Bay [San Francisco] sidewalks is a smelly, vermin-infested reminder of how easily we take for granted the idea that no matter what we throw away, there'll be some place to put it.

The reality is that the United States is awash in garbage, and we're rapidly running out of ways to dispose of it.

We Need More Space for Garbage

According to the Environmental Protection Agency, Americans generated more than 245 million tons of trash—or municipal solid waste in technical jargon—in 2005, the latest year for which national figures are available. That translates to roughly 4 1/2 pounds of garbage produced by every person every day.

And that, in turn, has resulted in a $52 billion industry dedicated to dumping, incinerating and recycling all the nasty, gooey, hinky, stinky stuff that we don't want.

"It's a very, very serious problem," said Syed Qasim, a professor of civil and environmental engineering at the University of Texas who specializes in waste management. "In many states, we are running out of room for all the garbage we produce."

Beyond space considerations, there's also the matter of potentially hazardous gases, such as methane, generated by rotting trash in landfills, not to mention toxic chemicals leaking into groundwater supplies.

We Generate Too Much Trash

"We have to cut down on the amount of garbage we generate," Qasim said.

Easier said than done. As many have observed, America is a throwaway society. Yes, we recycle. Yes, we compost. But by and large,

America's throwaway society has generated unprecedented amounts of electronic garbage.
Each American produces four and a half pounds of garbage a day.

we use things until we're done with them, and then we toss them in the trash.

At the same time, we buy our drinking water in little plastic bottles. We chuck out our computers and music players and other gizmos as soon as a cooler version comes along. We readily accept, and even desire, that the things we purchase come with multiple layers of packaging.

"Everything is throwaway," said Mark Murray, executive director of Californians Against Waste, a Sacramento advocacy group. "Everything is disposable."

This is one reason the trash is piling up so quickly in the East Bay. Waste-collection giant Waste Management locked out nearly 500 garbage truck drivers last week [July 2007] amid fears that union members were planning a strike. Replacement workers were brought in by the company, but the garbage has been accumulating too quickly for them to get it all off the sidewalks. Flies are buzzing around the heaps of black plastic garbage bags. They'll soon be spreading bacteria from the trash into people's homes, public health experts say.

Next will come ants. Then cockroaches. Then rats.

Hyper-consumerism Adds to the Trash Problem

To Murray, the problem isn't just the vast amounts of leftover food and household waste that we hand off to garbage collectors. It's the detritus of our hyper-consumerism. "We throw away last year's model because we just have to have this year's model," he said. "As a result, last year's model ends up in the waste stream."

Part of the blame for that, Murray said, rests with people who seldom give a thought to what happens when they discard something. But much of the responsibility, he said, lies with companies that have only one message for customers—buy, buy, buy.

"Manufacturers are in the business of selling more and more stuff," Murray observed. "They're constantly trying to get people to buy a new version, an upgraded version."

Jon Myers, director of public affairs for the state Integrated Waste Management Board, acknowledged that companies can be doing a lot more to reduce waste throughout California. But he said his agency, which oversees the 92 million tons of trash generated statewide each year, is already working closely with a variety of companies to show them how they can operate in a more environmentally friendly way without cutting into profits.

"The good news is that we're doing a lot of recycling and taking other steps to reduce waste," Myers said. "The bad news is that we're not doing enough."

FAST FACT

The organization Inform Inc. reports that 179,000 vehicles are used to haul away garbage in the United States.

We Need Creative Ways to Dispose of Trash

California has 157 permitted landfills, with just one more— Gregory Canyon near San Diego—in the works. The state also has one of the best track records for recycling garbage, with about 54 percent of trash being diverted away from landfills.

What's in America's Garbage?

Americans generate millions of tons of trash each year.

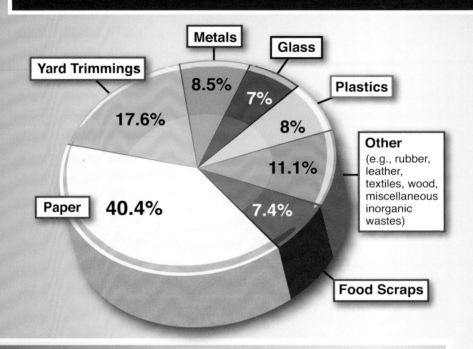

- **Metals** 8.5%
- **Glass** 7%
- **Plastics** 8%
- **Yard Trimmings** 17.6%
- **Paper** 40.4%
- **Other** (e.g., rubber, leather, textiles, wood, miscellaneous inorganic wastes) 11.1%
- **Food Scraps** 7.4%

Table of Trash Types and Percentages

Trash Type	Percentage	Tonnage
paper	40.4%	71.6 million tons
yard trimmings	17.6%	31.6 million tons
metals	8.5%	15.3 million tons
plastics	8.0%	14.4 million tons
food scraps	7.4%	13.2 million tons
glass	7.0%	12.5 million tons
other	11.1%	20.8 million tons

Taken from: U.S. Environmental Protection Agency. www.epa.gov/epaoswer/non-hw/reduce/catbook/what.htm.

Is that good enough? "Not even close," answered Myers.

The reason for his apprehension is that California's population is booming. By 2050, according to a state report issued this week, the population will soar to 60 million from 36 million now. "We're looking at that," Myers said, "and we're thinking, 'Wow, that's going to be a lot of trash.'"

One man's trash, of course, is another's treasure. Daniel Waldman, publisher of *MSW Management*, a California trade journal for waste-management professionals, said the garbage industry foresees new techniques and technologies to convert garbage into energy.

He also envisions businesses that profit by focusing on recycling and conservation. "This is a significant problem, but it's also a significant opportunity," Waldman said.

Murray at Californians Against Waste believes we have to be even more proactive. Part of his solution to our garbage woes is to build disposal costs into the retail price of consumer goods. You buy a computer, you'll pay up front for its eventual demise. Same with an iPod, or a pair of sneakers, or whatever.

"You're paying for it anyway," Murray said. "You're paying for it in your taxes. If we paid for it up front, maybe we'd make better purchasing decisions."

"Think of all the resources and energy that goes into all these products," he added. "We're just generating too much junk."

EVALUATING THE AUTHOR'S ARGUMENTS:

In this viewpoint Lazarus claims that Americans' addiction to shopping is at the heart of the nation's trash crisis. Consider the last five purchases you have made. What trash was associated with these products? How much packaging did the items come in? Did you recycle any trash associated with the product? Make a list of each item and its associated garbage. Then, state whether you agree with Lazarus's assertion that consumerism contributes to a trash problem.

We Are Not Running Out of Room for Garbage

Alan Caruba

"The nation's entire solid waste for the next 1,000 years could be buried in a single landfill 100 yards high and 35 miles square. We are not running out of land for landfills."

In the following viewpoint author Alan Caruba argues there is plenty of space in America to build landfills for the nation's garbage. The problem, in Caruba's opinion, is that environmentalists have falsely claimed that landfills and incinerators are unsafe. As a result, thousands of them have been closed, and it has become more difficult and costly to open new ones. But landfills are not dangerous, according to the author: They provide a cost-effective way to deal with garbage, and when they are filled can provide some of the best, safest real estate around. Caruba urges Americans not to believe the hype that recycling garbage is better than putting it in a landfill. To the contrary, he says that recycling is more expensive and wasteful in its own way. Caruba concludes that landfills and incinerators are good, safe ways to get rid of garbage, and as long as they are properly funded, they will provide plenty of space for American garbage for hundreds of years to come.

Alan Caruba, "The Utter Waste of Recycling," CNSNews.com, January 17, 2003. Reproduced by permission of the author.

Alan Caruba is a writer who critiques subjects such as environmentalism, Islam, and global warming. He writes regularly for CNSNews.com, from which this viewpoint is taken.

AS YOU READ, CONSIDER THE FOLLOWING QUESTIONS:
1. Who are the "Greens" and what does Caruba blame them for?
2. According to Caruba, what types of property have landfills been converted into?
3. According to the author, how much money can New York City save by not requiring recycling?

Twice a month I have to bundle my newspapers and take boxes with glass and plastic items down to the curb to be removed and, one assumes, recycled. This does not include the two other pickups for what is presumably just plain old garbage.

Recycling Is Wasteful and Ineffective

I am old enough to remember when a person just threw all of this stuff into the garbage can to be taken away. It involved two less trips and a smaller bill from the "waste management" company.

Ask yourself about the utility of recycling. Glass is made from sand. The Earth is not running out of sand. Newspapers, when buried, stay intact for decades and, when burned, become mere ashes. Recycling plastic requires as much or more energy than that used to produce it. Its uses, however, are extraordinary, contributing to a healthier lifestyle for everyone. So, why recycle?

In 1998, it cost Americans $36 billion to get rid of 210 million tons of municipal waste. It probably costs more today. Part of that multi-billion cost is the additional element of recycling requirements. It's not like you have a choice. New York City publishes a brochure on recycling that says bluntly "It's the law."

There is no question that Americans produce a lot of garbage. In the past we buried or burned it, but that was before the environmentalists, Greens, began a campaign that would have us believe there was no room left for landfills, that landfills were inherently a "hazard," and that incinerators were no better because of what came out of the

Methods of Trash Disposal

Most of the world's waste is deposited in landfills.

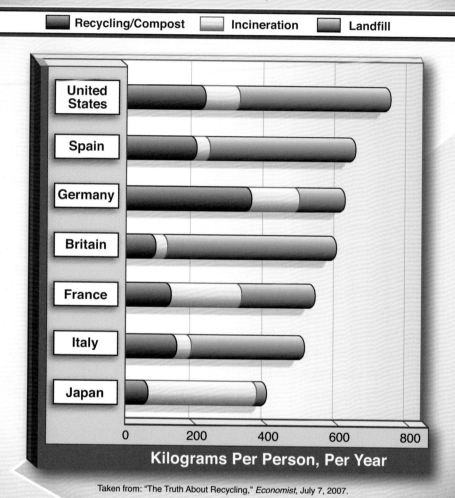

■ Recycling/Compost   ☐ Incineration   ■ Landfill

Kilograms Per Person, Per Year

Taken from: "The Truth About Recycling," *Economist*, July 7, 2007.

smokestack. All of a sudden, it became very costly to get rid of the garbage where, before, it was no big deal.

Closing Landfills Is a Mistake

The result of the Green lies about garbage was the closing of thousands of landfills around the nation and the increased difficulty of opening new ones. One effort in New Jersey to build a new incinerator ended up a financial nightmare for investors when the courts ruled that haulers could not be compelled by law to bring the garbage to the incinerator, especially if it was cheaper to dump it somewhere else. The problem is not that we have more garbage. The problem is we have fewer places to bury and burn it. For that you can thank the Greens. This is something to think about every time you separate your glass and plastic or bundle your newspapers.

You may feel you are doing something noble for the environment, but you are paying more for that privilege and the odds are the stuff is being buried and burned just the same. The market for anything recycled often proves unprofitable because the cost of recycling does not justify itself.

There Is Enough Space for Garbage

One scholar, A. Clark Wiseman of Spokane's Gonzaga University, calculated that, at the current rate of solid waste generation, the nation's entire solid waste for the next 1,000 years could be buried in a single landfill 100 yards high and 35 miles square.

We are not running out of land for landfills. We have run into the lie that they are unsafe. The truth is that landfills have been routinely converted into valuable property once filled. In California there are a number of golf courses that were former landfills. In New Jersey, there are malls and corporate campuses.

In July of last year, New York City suspended the collection of plastic and beverage cartons for a year and the collection of glass for two years. Said the Mayor, "This temporary suspension will save the City an estimated $40 million." Now do the math. If New York can save $40 million by not requiring recycling, imagine the billions that could be saved by cities and suburbs coast to coast? You could renovate every school in America with those funds.

> **FAST FACT**
>
> According to the Competitive Enterprise Institute, 60 percent of landfills pose a 1 in a billion risk of causing cancer, while only 17 percent pose a 1 in a million risk.

Laws That Are Garbage

In the end, if recycling was cost-efficient why is it necessary to pass laws to *force* people to separate and bundle stuff that could just as easily be tossed out with the rest of the garbage? That's how environmentalism works. It creates a Big Lie and then sets about getting laws passed to mandate it. Years later, states, cities, communities, and just ordinary people begin to ask, "Why are we doing this?" and the answer is, "It's the law."

The viewpoint's author thinks that the United States has plenty of room for landfills and that recycling is not cost-efficient.

It wasn't always the law. There was a time when landfills were understood to be a perfectly sensible way to get rid of the garbage. Incinerators, too. But that was before the Greens decided recycling was a dandy way to make everyone think that throwing out the garbage was yet another "hazard," "danger," and "threat" to Mother Earth. To which I say, "That's just garbage!"

EVALUATING THE AUTHORS' ARGUMENTS:

In this viewpoint Caruba argues that there is enough space to dispose of all the garbage generated by Americans. How do you think the author of the preceding viewpoint, David Lazarus, might respond to this argument? Explain your answer using evidence from both texts.

Garbage in the Ocean Is a Serious Threat

Greenpeace

> *"The scale of contamination of the marine environment by plastic debris is vast."*

In the following viewpoint the environmental organization Greenpeace contends that garbage in the ocean, or marine debris, is a serious problem that threatens both humans and wildlife. Garbage in the ocean—such as plastic bags, nets, and ropes—traps animals and birds, injuring or killing them. Other animals ingest marine debris, hurting themselves and passing toxic chemicals up the food chain. Still other animals use plastic debris to hitch rides to areas of the ocean where they do not naturally live, creating problems. Boats and ships may also get entangled in marine debris, raising safety concerns and incurring ship repair costs. The author further suggests that trash in the ocean may cause a loss of tourism dollars because people do not want to recreate in polluted water. For all these reasons, Greenpeace concludes that ocean garbage is a serious problem, one that will require education, responsibility, and action to reduce the threat.

Greenpeace is a nonprofit organization that uses peaceful, direct action to bring attention to global environmental problems.

Michelle Allsopp, Adam Walters, David Santillo, and Paul Johnston, *Plastic Debris in the World's Oceans,* Amsterdam, The Netherlands: Greenpeace International, 2006. Reproduced by permission.

AS YOU READ, CONSIDER THE FOLLOWING QUESTIONS:
1. How many species have suffered from entanglement or ingestion of marine debris, according to Greenpeace?
2. What are the four main sources of marine debris, as reported by
   the author?
3. What are "alien species," and how does marine debris affect them?

It is probably a common conception that marine debris consists of just a few pieces of rubbish scattered along the strand line of beaches and is of no harm to anyone. Unfortunately this is not the case. Marine debris has become a pervasive pollution problem affecting all of the world's oceans. It is known to be the cause of injuries and deaths of numerous marine animals and birds, either because they become entangled in it or they mistake it for prey and eat it.

Plastic and synthetic materials are the most common types of marine debris and cause the most problems for marine animals and birds. At least 267 different species are known to have suffered from entanglement or ingestion of marine debris including seabirds, turtles, seals, sea lions, whales and fish.

The scale of contamination of the marine environment by plastic debris is vast. It is found floating in all the world's oceans, everywhere from polar regions to the equator. The seabed, especially near to coastal regions, is also contaminated—predominantly with plastic bags. Plastic is also ubiquitous on beaches everywhere from populous regions to the shores of very remote uninhabited islands.

Attempts to address the problem of marine debris range from international legislation to prevent shipping from dumping plastic at sea and campaigns to prevent losses due to poor industrial practice to beach and seabed clean-up operations and public awareness campaigns. Plastic debris originates from a wide and diverse range of sources. Estimates suggest that much of what is found at sea originates on the land. The effect of coastal littering and dumping is compounded by vectors such as rivers and storm drains discharging litter from inland urban areas. It is the very properties that make plastics so useful, their stability and resistance to degradation, that causes them to be so problematic after they have served their purpose. These materials persist in the environment and are not readily degraded or processed by natural biological mechanisms. However plastics in the ocean are weathered; broken up either mechanically or by the action of sunlight into smaller and smaller fragments. Eventually, fragments are reduced to tiny pieces the size of grains of sand. These particles have been found suspended in seawater and on the seabed in sediments. Even such tiny particles may be causing harm to the marine environment since they have been shown to be ingested by small sea creatures and may concentrate persistent organic pollutants (POPs) present in the seas. . . .

FAST FACT

According to the UN Environment Programme, every square mile of ocean contains forty-six thousand pieces of floating plastic.

Sources of Marine Debris

It has been estimated that around 80% of marine debris is from land-based sources and the remaining 20% is from ocean based sources. The sources can be categorised into four major groups:

- Tourism-related litter at the coast: this includes litter left by beach goers such as food and beverage packaging, cigarettes and plastic beach toys.
- Sewage-related debris: this includes water from storm drains and combined sewer overflows which discharge waste water directly into the sea or rivers during heavy rainfall. These waste waters carry with them garbage such as street litter, condoms and syringes.
- Fishing-related debris: this includes fishing lines and nets, fishing pots and strapping bands from bait boxes that are lost accidentally by commercial fishing boats or are deliberately dumped into the ocean
- Wastes from ships and boats: this includes garbage which is accidentally or deliberately dumped overboard.

Huge volumes of non-organic wastes, including plastics and synthetics, are produced in more developed, industrialised countries. Conversely, in less developed and more rural economies, generally a much smaller amount of these non-biodegradable persistent wastes are produced. However, in the future, as less developed countries become more industrialised, it is likely that they will also produce more plastic and synthetic wastes and this will increase further the threat of pollution of the marine environment.

Harm to Marine Wildlife

Countless marine animals and sea birds become entangled in marine debris or ingest it. This can cause them serious harm and often results in their death.

Entanglement in Marine Debris

Marine debris which is known to cause entanglement includes derelict fishing gear such as nets and mono-filament line and also six-pack rings and fishing bait box strapping bands. This debris can cause death by drowning, suffocation, strangulation, starvation through reduced

Plastic bag debris is vast in the world's oceans and has become a serious problem. According to Greenpeace, the bags do not degrade and cause harm to the marine environment.

feeding efficiency, and injuries. Particularly affected are seals and sea lions, probably due to their very inquisitive nature of investigating objects in their environment. Entanglement rates in these animals of up to 7.9% of a population have been recorded. Furthermore, in some instances entanglement is a threat to the recovery of already reduced population sizes. An estimated 58% of seal and sea lion species are known to have been affected by entanglement including the Hawaiian monk seal, Australian sea lions, New Zealand fur seals and species in the Southern Ocean.

Whales, dolphins, porpoises, turtles, manatees and seabirds have all been reported to have suffered from entanglement. Many different species of whale and turtle have been reported to have been tangled in plastic. Manatees have been found with scars or missing flippers due to entanglement. 51 species of seabirds are also known to have been affected. Derelict fishing gear also causes damage to coral reefs when nets or lines get snagged by the reef and break it off. . . .

Ingestion of Marine Debris

Ingestion of marine debris is known to particularly affect sea turtles and seabirds but is also a problem for marine mammals and fish. Ingestion is generally thought to occur because the marine debris is mistaken for prey. Most of that erroneously ingested is plastic. Different types of debris are ingested by marine animals including plastic bags, plastic pellets and fragments of plastic that have been broken up from larger items. The biggest threat from ingestion occurs when it blocks the digestive tract, or fills the stomach, resulting in malnutrition, starvation and potentially death.

Studies have shown that a high proportion (about 50 to 80%) of sea turtles found dead are known to have ingested marine debris. This can have a negative impact on turtle populations. In young turtles, a major problem is dietary dilution in which debris takes up some of the gut capacity and threatens their ability to take on necessary quantities of food.

For seabirds, 111 out of 312 species are known to have ingested debris and it can affect a large percentage of a population (up to 80%). Moreover, plastic debris is also known to be passed to the chicks in regurgitated food from their parents. One harmful effect from plastic ingestion in birds is weight loss due for example to a falsely sated

Marine Life Is Threatened

Penguins, whales, and turtles are just a few of the marine species that are harmed or killed by ocean garbage.

Species Group	Total number of species worldwide	Number and percentage of species with entanglement records	Number and percentage of species with ingestion records
Sea Turtles	7	6 (86%)	6 (86%)
Seabirds	312	51 (16%)	111 (36%)
Penguins	16	6 (38%)	1 (6%)
Grebes	19	2 (10%)	0
Albatrosses, Petrels, and Shearwaters	99	10 (10%)	62 (63%)
Pelicans, Boobies, Gannets, Cormorants, Frigatebirds, and Tropicbirds	51	11 (22%)	8 (16%)
Shorebirds, Skuas, Gulls, Terns, Auks	122	22 (18%)	40 (33%)
Other birds	–	5	0
Marine Mammals	115	32 (28%)	26 (23%)
Baleen Whales	10	6 (60%)	2 (20%)
Toothed Whales	65	5 (8%)	21 (32%)
Fur Seals and Sea Lions	14	11 (79%)	1 (7%)
True Seals	19	8 (42%)	1 (5%)
Manatees and Dugongs	4	1 (25%)	1 (25%)
Sea Otter	1	1 (100%)	0
Fish	–	34	33
Crustaceans	–	8	0
Squid	–	0	1
Species Total	–	136	177

Taken from: Greenpeace.

appetite and failure to put on adequate fat stores for migration and reproduction.

Potential Invasion of Alien Species

Plastic debris which floats on the oceans can act as rafts for small sea creatures to grow and travel on. Plastic can travel for long distances and therefore there is a possibility that marine animals and plants may travel to areas where they are non-native. Plastic with different sorts of animals and plants have been found in the oceans in areas remote from their source. This represents a potential threat for the marine environment should an alien species become established. It is postulated that the slow speed at which plastic debris crosses oceans makes it an ideal vehicle for this. The organisms have plenty of time to adapt to different water and climatic conditions.

EVALUATING THE AUTHOR'S ARGUMENTS:

The author of this viewpoint is Greenpeace, an environmental activist organization. Does knowing this background influence your opinion of the author's argument? If so, in what way?

The Threat of Ocean Garbage Has Been Exaggerated

Alexi Mostrous

"There is no scientific evidence to show that the [plastic] bags pose any direct threat to marine mammals."

In the following viewpoint author Alexi Mostrous argues that the threat of ocean garbage has been exaggerated. Specifically, he claims that plastic bags are not a threat to marine animals as some environmentalists have claimed. Mostrous contends that plastic bags in the ocean have become demonized as a result of environmentalist efforts to exaggerate their threat and of officials who have misinterpreted several key studies on marine debris. In reality, says Mostrous, plastic bags rarely cause the entanglement of animals and almost never cause their death. For these reasons, Mostrous concludes that plastic bags pose a minimal threat to the marine environment and that banning them will only create hardship for consumers.

Mostrous writes regularly for the London *Times*, from which this viewpoint is taken.

Alexi Mostrous, "Series of Blunders Turned the Plastic Bag into Global Villain," *Times* (London), March 8, 2008. Reproduced by permission.

AS YOU READ, CONSIDER THE FOLLOWING QUESTIONS:
  1. Who is Lord Taverne, and how does he figure into the author's argument?
  2. Name five animals that the author reports are not impacted by plastic bags.
  3. What percent of landfill waste is composed of plastic bags, as reported by the author?

Scientists and environmentalists have attacked a global campaign to ban plastic bags which they say is based on flawed science and exaggerated claims.

Plastic Bags Pose a Minimal Threat to Marine Animals

The widely stated accusation that the bags kill 100,000 animals and a million seabirds every year [is] false, experts have told *The Times*. They pose only a minimal threat to most marine species, including seals, whales, dolphins and seabirds.

[British prime minister] Gordon Brown announced last month [February 2008] that he would force supermarkets to charge for the bags, saying that they were "one of the most visible symbols of environmental waste". Retailers and some pressure groups, including the Campaign to Protect Rural England, threw their support behind him.

But scientists, politicians and marine experts attacked the Government for joining a "bandwagon" based on poor science. Lord Taverne, the chairman of Sense about Science, said: "The Government is irresponsible to jump on a bandwagon that has no base in scientific evidence. This is one of many examples where you get bad science leading to bad decisions which are counter-productive. Attacking plastic bags makes people feel good but it doesn't achieve anything."

Campaigners say that plastic bags pollute coastlines and waterways, killing or injuring birds and livestock on land and, in the oceans, destroying vast numbers of seabirds, seals, turtles and whales. However, *The Times* has established that there is no scientific evidence to show that the bags pose any direct threat to marine mammals.

They "don't figure" in the majority of cases where animals die from marine debris, said David Laist, the author of a seminal 1997 study on the subject. Most deaths were caused when creatures became caught up in waste produce. "Plastic bags don't figure in entanglement," he said. "The main culprits are fishing gear, ropes, lines and strapping bands. Most mammals are too big to get caught up in a plastic bag."

He added: "The impact of bags on whales, dolphins, porpoises and seals ranges from nil for most species to very minor for perhaps a few species. For birds, plastic bags are not a problem either."

Getting the Facts Right

The central claim of campaigners is that the bags kill more than 100,000 marine mammals and one million seabirds every year. However, this figure is based on a misinterpretation of a 1987 Canadian study in Newfoundland, which found that, between 1981 and 1984, more than 100,000 marine mammals, including birds, were killed by discarded nets. The Canadian study did not mention plastic bags.

Fifteen years later in 2002, when the Australian Government commissioned a report into the effects of plastic bags, its authors misquoted the Newfoundland study, mistakenly attributing the deaths to "plastic bags".

The figure was latched on to by conservationists as proof that the bags were killers. For four years the "typo" remained uncorrected. It was only in 2006 that the authors altered the report, replacing "plastic bags" with "plastic debris". But they admitted: "The actual numbers of animals killed annually by plastic bag litter is nearly impossible to determine."

In a postscript to the correction they admitted that the original Canadian study had referred to fishing tackle, not plastic debris, as the threat to the marine environment. Regardless, the erroneous claim has become the keystone of a widening campaign to demonise plastic bags.

David Santillo, a marine biologist at Greenpeace, told *The Times* that bad science was undermining the Government's case for banning the bags. "It's very unlikely that many animals are killed by plastic bags," he said. "The evidence shows just the opposite. We are not going to solve the problem of waste by focusing on plastic bags. It doesn't do the Government's case any favours if you've got statements being made that aren't supported by the scientific literature

Plastic bag debris fills up a landfill. The viewpoint's author thinks that the impact of plastic bags in the ocean is a minimal threat to marine species.

that's out there. With larger mammals it's fishing gear that's the big problem. On a global basis plastic bags aren't an issue. It would be great if statements like these weren't made."

Geoffrey Cox, a Tory member of the Commons Environment Select Committee, said: "I don't like plastic bags and I certainly support restricting their use, but plainly it's extremely important that before we take any steps we should rely on accurate information. It is bizarre that any campaign should be endorsed on the basis of a mistranslation. Gordon Brown should get his facts right."

Focusing on the Actual Problem

A 1968 study of albatross carcasses found that 90 per cent contained some form of plastic but only two birds had ingested part of a plastic bag.

Professor Geoff Boxshall, a marine biologist at the Natural History Museum, said: "I've never seen a bird killed by a plastic bag. Other forms of plastic in the ocean are much more damaging. Only a very small proportion is caused by bags."

Plastic particles known as nurdles, dumped in the sea by industrial companies, form a much greater threat as they can be easily consumed by birds and animals. Many British groups are now questioning whether a ban on bags would cost consumers more than the environmental benefits.

Charlie Mayfield, chairman of retailer John Lewis, said that tackling packaging waste and reducing carbon emissions were far more important goals. "We don't see reducing the use of plastic bags as our biggest priority," he said. "Of all the waste that goes to landfill, 20 percent is household waste and 0.3 percent is plastic bags." John Lewis added that a scheme in Ireland had reduced plastic bag usage, but sales of bin liners had increased 400 percent.

EVALUATING THE AUTHOR'S ARGUMENTS:

Alexi Mostrous quotes from several sources to support the points he makes in this viewpoint. Make a list of all the people he quotes, including their credentials and the nature of their comments. Then, analyze his sources—are they credible? Are they well qualified to speak on this subject?

"Once aloft, stray bags cartwheel down city streets, alight in trees, billow from fences like flags, clog storm drains, wash into rivers and bays and even end up in the ocean, washed out to sea."

Plastic Bags Are a Serious Environmental Hazard

Katharine Mieszkowski

In the following viewpoint author Katharine Mieszkowski argues that plastic bags pose a serious environmental threat. She claims that thousands of pieces of plastic from bags end up in the ocean, landfills, streams, lakes, rivers, and other open spaces each year. Mieszkowski says one reason why plastic bags are so dangerous for the environment is because they contain lead, a toxic substance that is leaked into environments polluted with plastic bags. Another reason is because plastic bags take centuries to break down, meaning they will long outlive the people who used them. The author discusses how various plastic bag recycling efforts have not been very successful because consumers are not willing to bring their plastic bags into recycling centers and because recycling plastic bags into other bags is not cost-effective. She concludes that reusing the same bags over and over while shopping is the best way to minimize plastic trash pollution in the environment.

Katharine Mieszkowski, "Plastic Bags Are Killing Us," Salon.com, August 10, 2007. This article first appeared in Salon.com, at http://www.salon.com. An online version remains in the Salon archives. Reprinted with permission.

Mieszkowski is a senior writer for Salon.com. She writes about business, technology, and the environment.

AS YOU READ, CONSIDER THE FOLLOWING QUESTIONS:
1. What are plastic bags made from?
2. According to the author, how many plastic bags do Americans throw away every year?
3. What percent of plastic bags does the United States recycle, according to the author?

Aug. 10, 2007 | OAKLAND, Calif. — On a foggy Tuesday morning, kids out of school for summer break are learning to sail on the waters of Lake Merritt. A great egret hunts for fish, while dozens of cormorants perch, drying their wings. But we're not here to bird-watch or go boating. Twice a week volunteers with the Lake Merritt Institute gather on these shores of the nation's oldest national wildlife refuge to fish trash out of the water, and one of their prime targets is plastic bags. Armed with gloves and nets with long handles, like the kind you'd use to fish leaves out of a backyard swimming pool, we take to the shores to seek our watery prey.

Dr. Richard Bailey, executive director of the institute, is most concerned about the bags that get waterlogged and sink to the bottom. "We have a lot of animals that live on the bottom: shrimp, shellfish, sponges,—he says. "It's like you're eating at your dinner table and somebody comes along and throws a plastic tarp over your dinner table and you."

This morning, a turtle feeds serenely next to a half submerged Walgreens bag. The bag looks ghostly, ethereal even, floating, as if in some kind of purgatory suspended between its briefly useful past and its none-too-promising future. A bright blue bag floats just out of reach, while a duck cruises by. Here's a Ziploc bag, there a Safeway bag. In a couple of hours, I fish more than two dozen plastic bags out of the lake with my net, along with cigarette butts, candy wrappers and a soccer ball. As we work, numerous passersby on the popular trail that circles the urban lake shout their thanks, which is an undeniable boost. Yet I can't help being struck that our efforts represent a tiny drop in the ocean. If there's one thing we know about these plastic bags, it's that there are billions and billions more where they came from.

The plastic bag is an icon of convenience culture, by some estimates the single most ubiquitous consumer item on Earth, numbering in the trillions. They're made from petroleum or natural gas with all the attendant environmental impacts of harvesting fossil fuels. One recent study found that the inks and colorants used on some bags contain lead, a toxin. Every year, Americans throw away some 100 billion plastic bags after they've been used to transport a prescription home from the drugstore or a quart of milk from the grocery store. It's equivalent to dumping nearly 12 million barrels of oil.

Only 1 percent of plastic bags are recycled worldwide—about 2 percent in the U.S.—and the rest, when discarded, can persist for centuries. They can spend eternity in landfills, but that's not always the case. "They're so aerodynamic that even when they're properly disposed of in a trash can they can still blow away and become litter," says Mark Murray, executive director of Californians Against Waste. It's as litter that plastic bags have the most baleful effect. And we're not talking about your everyday eyesore.

Once aloft, stray bags cartwheel down city streets, alight in trees, billow from fences like flags, clog storm drains, wash into rivers and bays and even end up in the ocean, washed out to sea. Bits of plastic bags have been found in the nests of albatrosses in the remote Midway Islands. Floating bags can look all too much like tasty jellyfish to hungry marine critters. According to the Blue Ocean Society for Marine Conservation, more than a million birds and 100,000 marine mammals and sea turtles die every year from eating or getting entangled in plastic. The conservation group estimates that 50 percent of all marine litter is some form of plastic. There are 46,000 pieces of plastic litter floating in every square mile of ocean, according to the United Nations Environment Programme. In the Northern Pacific Gyre, a great vortex of ocean currents, there's now a swirling mass of plastic trash about 1,000 miles off the coast of California, which spans an area that's twice the size of Texas, including fragments of plastic bags. There's six times as much plastic as biomass, including plankton and jellyfish, in the gyre. "It's an endless stream of incessant plastic particles everywhere you look," says Dr. Marcus Eriksen, director of

Cities like San Francisco and Oakland, California, have begun plastic bag recycling efforts and have banned their use in large grocery stores.

education and research for the Algalita Marine Research Foundation, which studies plastics in the marine environment. "Fifty or 60 years ago, there was no plastic out there."

Following the lead of countries like Ireland, Bangladesh, South Africa, Thailand and Taiwan, some U.S. cities are striking back against what they see as an expensive, wasteful and unnecessary mess. This year, San Francisco and Oakland outlawed the use of plastic bags in large grocery stores and pharmacies, permitting only paper bags with at least 40 percent recycled content or otherwise compostable bags. The bans have not taken effect yet, but already the city of Oakland is being sued by an association of plastic bag manufacturers calling itself the Coalition to Support Plastic Bag Recycling. Meanwhile, other communities across the country, including Santa Monica, Calif., New Haven, Conn., Annapolis, Md., and Portland, Ore., are considering taking drastic legislative action against the bags. In Ireland, a now 22-cent tax on plastic bags has slashed their use by more than 90 percent since 2002. In flood-prone Bangladesh, where plastic bags choked drainage systems, the bags have been banned since 2002.

The problem with plastic bags isn't just where they end up, it's that they never seem to end. "All the plastic that has been made is still around in smaller and smaller pieces," says Stephanie Barger, executive director of the Earth Resource Foundation, which has undertaken a Campaign Against the Plastic Plague. Plastic doesn't biodegrade. That means unless they've been incinerated—a noxious proposition—every plastic bag you've ever used in your entire life, including all those bags that the newspaper arrives in on your doorstep, even on cloudless days when there isn't a sliver of a chance of rain, still exists in some form, even fragmented bits, and will exist long after you're dead.

Grand efforts are under way to recycle plastic bags, but so far those efforts have resulted mostly in a mass of confusion. A tour of Recycle Central in San Francisco makes it easy to see why. The plant is a Willie Wonka factory of refuse. Located on a bay pier with a stunning view of the downtown skyline, some 700 tons of discarded annual reports, Rolling Rock bottles, Diet Coke cans, Amazon.com cardboard boxes, Tide plastic detergent bottles and StarKist tuna fish cans surge into this warehouse every weekday, dumped from trucks into a great clattering, shifting mound. The building tinkles and thumps with the sound of thousands of pounds of glass, aluminum, paper, plastic and cardboard

FAST FACT

According to the Sierra Club, one less grocery bag per person in New York City alone would reduce waste by 109 tons and save $11,000 in disposal costs.

knocking together, as all this detritus passes through a dizzying network of conveyor belts, spinning disks, magnets and gloved human
hands to emerge as 16 different sorted, recyclable commodities, baled
up by the ton to be shipped or trucked away and made into something new again. It's one way that the city of San Francisco manages
to divert some 69 percent of its waste from landfills. But this city's
vaunted recycling program, which is so advanced that it can collect
coffee grounds and banana peels from urbanites' apartment kitchens
and transform them into compost used to grow grapes in Napa Valley
vineyards, simply cannot master the plastic bag.

Ask John Jurinek, the plant manager at Recycle Central, what's
wrong with plastic bags and he has a one-word answer: "Everything."
Plastic bags, of which San Franciscans use some 180 million per year,
cannot be recycled here. Yet the hopeful arrow symbol emblazoned
on the bags no doubt inspires lots of residents to toss their used ones
into the blue recycling bin, feeling good that they've done the right
thing. But that symbol on all kinds of plastic items by no means guar-
antees they can be recycled curbside. (The plastic bags collected at the
recycling plant are trucked to the regular dump.) By chucking their
plastic bags in the recycling, what those well-meaning San Franciscans
have done is throw a plastic wrench into the city's grand recycling
factory. If you want to recycle a plastic bag it's better to bring it back
to the store where you got it.

As the great mass of recyclables moves past the initial sort deck on
a series of spinning disks, stray plastic bags clog the machinery. It's
such a problem that one machine is shut down while a worker wearing
kneepads and armed with a knife spends an hour climbing precari-
ously on the disks to cut the bags out, yielding a Medusa's hair-mass
of wrenched and twisted plastic. In the middle of the night, when the
vast sorting operation grinds to a halt to prepare for the next 700-ton
day, two workers will spend hours at this dirty job.

Some states are attacking the recycling problem by trying to
encourage shoppers to take the bags back to grocery stores. California
requires large grocery stores and pharmacies that distribute the bags
known in the trade as T-shirt bags -- those common polyethylene bags
with two handles, usually made from petroleum or natural gas—to
take them back for recycling, and to print instructions on the bags
to encourage shoppers to return them to the stores. San Francisco

Environment Department spokesperson Mark Westlund, who can see plastic bags lodged in the trees on Market Street from his second-story office window, is skeptical about the state's ability to get shoppers to take back their bags. "We've had in store recycling in San Francisco for over 10 years, and it's never really been successful," says Westlund, who estimates that the city achieved only a 1 percent recycling rate of plastic bags at the stores. "People have to pack up the bags, bring them into the store and drop them off. I think you'd be more inclined to bring your own bag than do that."

Regardless, polyethylene plastic bags are recyclable, says Howie Fendley, a senior environmental chemist for MBDC, an ecological design firm. "It's a matter of getting the feedstock to the point where a recycler can economically justify taking those bags and recycling them. The problem is they're mostly air. There has to be a system in place where they get a nice big chunk of polyethylene that can be mechanically ground, melted and then re-extruded."

So far that system nationwide consists mainly of supermarkets and superstores like Wal-Mart voluntarily stockpiling the bags brought back in by conscientious shoppers, and selling them to recyclers or plastic brokers, who in turn sell them to recyclers. In the U.S., one company buys half of the used plastic bags available on the open market in the United States, using about 1.5 billion plastic bags per year. That's Trex, based in Winchester, Va., which makes composite decking out of the bags and recycled wood. It takes some 2,250 plastic bags to make a single 16-foot-long, 2-inch-by-6-inch plank. It might feel good to buy decking made out of something that otherwise could have choked a sea turtle, but not so fast. That use is not an example of true recycling, points out Carol Misseldine, sustainability coordinator for the city of Oakland. "We're not recycling plastic bags into plastic bags," she says. "They're being downcycled, meaning that they're being put into another product that itself can never be recycled."

Unlike a glass beer bottle or an aluminum can, it's unusual that a plastic bag is made back into another plastic bag, because it's typically more expensive than just making a new plastic bag. After all, the major appeal of plastic bags to stores is that they're much cheaper than paper. Plastic bags cost grocery stores under 2 cents per bag, while paper goes for 4 to 6 cents and compostable bags 9 to 14 cents. However, says Eriksen from the Algalita Marine Research

Foundation, "The long-term cost of having these plastic bags blowing across our landscape, across our beaches and accumulating in the northern Pacific far outweighs the short-term loss to a few."

Of course, shoppers could just bring their own canvas bags, and avoid the debate altogether. The California bag recycling law also requires stores to sell reusable bags. Yet it will be a sad irony if outlawing the bags, as San Francisco and Oakland have, doesn't inspire shoppers to bring their own canvas bags, but simply sends them to paper bags, which come with their own environmental baggage. In fact, plastic bags were once thought to be an ecologically friendly alternative to cutting down trees to make paper ones. It takes 14 million trees to produce the 10 billion paper grocery bags used every year by Americans, according to the Natural Resources Defense Council. Yet suggesting that plastic bags made out of petroleum are a better choice burns up Barger from the Earth Resources Foundation. "People say, 'I'm using plastic. I'm saving trees,'" he says. "But have you ever seen what Shell, Mobil and Chevron are doing down in the rain forests to get oil?"

Gordon Bennett, an executive in the San Francisco Bay chapter of the Sierra Club, agrees. "The fundamental thing about trees is that if you manage them properly they're a renewable resource," he says. "I haven't heard about the oil guys growing more oil lately." Still, as the plastic bag industry never tires of pointing out, paper bags are heavier than plastic bags, so they take more fossil fuels to transport. Some life cycle assessments have put plastic bags out ahead of paper, when it comes to energy and waste in the manufacturing process. But paper bags with recycled content, like those soon to be required in San Francisco and Oakland, use less energy and produce less waste than those made from virgin paper.

The only salient answer to paper or plastic is neither. Bring a reusable canvas bag, says Darby Hoover, a senior resource specialist for the Natural Resources Defense Council. However, if you have to make a choice between the two, she recommends taking whichever bag you're more likely to reuse the most times, since, like many products, the production of plastic or paper bags has the biggest environmental impact, not the disposal of them. "Reusing is a better option because it avoids the purchase of another product."

Some stores, like IKEA, have started trying to get customers to bring their own bags by charging them 5 cents per plastic bag. The

Swedish furniture company donates the proceeds from the bag sales to a conservation group. Another solution just might be fashion. Bringing your own bag—or BYOB as Whole Foods dubs it—is the latest eco-chic statement. When designer Anya Hindmarch's "I am not a plastic bag" bag hit stores in Taiwan, there was so much demand for the limited-edition bag that the riot police had to be called in to control a stampede, which sent 30 people to the hospital.

EVALUATING THE AUTHOR'S ARGUMENTS:

The author of this viewpoint suggests that bringing a reusable canvas bag for shopping instead of using paper or plastic bags will help eliminate environmental waste. How effective do you think that solution will be? Do you think it will help solve the trash problem? If yes, explain your reasoning. If no, suggest another way to reduce the threat of plastic bag litter.

Viewpoint 6

Plastic Bags Are Not an Environmental Hazard

Progressive Bag Alliance

"Plastic bags are 100% recyclable and for all environmental impacts related to air emissions, water emissions and solid waste—those of paper bags are significantly greater than that of plastic grocery bags."

In the following viewpoint the Progressive Bag Alliance debunks myths about plastic bags, arguing they do not pose a threat to the environment. They claim that compared to paper bags, plastic bags require less energy to produce, generate fewer emissions, and consume less fossil fuels. In the author's opinion, plastic bags can and should be recycled, and these programs successfully reduce the negative impact plastic bags have on the environment. Indeed, the author reports that plastic bags are 100 percent recyclable, but people do not recycle them enough because recycling programs are not available in all stores. The author concludes that plastic bags are environmentally friendly, cost-effective products that are both important to and safe for modern society.

The Progressive Bag Alliance, founded in 2005 and renamed the Progressive Bag Affiliates (PBA) in 2008, is a group of

"Top 10 Myths About Plastic Grocery Bags," Progressive Bag Alliance. www.plasticsindustry.org. Accessed May 7, 2008. © Copyright May 7, 2008 The Society of the Plastics Industry, Inc. All rights reserved. Distributed by Gale/Cengage with the permission of SPI.

American plastic bag manufacturers who fight against laws banning plastic grocery bags.

AS YOU READ, CONSIDER THE FOLLOWING QUESTIONS:
1. What are New Jersey, New York, and some cities in California opting to do with plastic bags instead of banning them, according to the author?
2. According to the author, how much less energy does it take to recycle a pound of plastic versus a pound of paper?
3. Name three consumer products the author says can be made from recycled plastic bags.

Myth #1: Plastic bag bans are spreading like wildfire across the country.

Fact: No. In fact, plastic bags have not been banned anywhere, not even in San Francisco. San Francisco is requiring that consumers use compostable plastic bags instead of 100% recyclable bags. Contrary to popular belief, there is a growing movement to increase access to recycled plastic bags—not eliminate them. New Jersey, Connecticut, and cities in California have all taken recent action to table legislation that would ban certain types of plastic bags and instead are now looking to implement plastic bag recycling programs.

Myth #2: Paper grocery bags are a better environmental choice than plastic bags.

Fact: Plastic bags are 100% recyclable and for all environmental impacts related to air emissions, water emissions and solid waste—those of paper bags are significantly greater than that of plastic grocery bags:

- Plastic bags use 40% less energy to produce and generate 80% less solid waste than paper
- Paper bags generate 70% more emissions, and 50 times more water pollutants than plastic bags.
- Even paper bags made from 100% recycled fiber use more fossil fuels than plastic bags

Myth #3: Plastic bags are the largest component of landfills and the primary component of litter.

Fact: The item most frequently encountered in landfills is paper—on average, it accounts for more than 40% of a landfill's contents. Newspapers alone take up as much as 13% of landfill space.

Cigarette butts, chewing gum, and candy wrappers account for about 95% of all litter in the English-speaking world. Education, as well as responsible use and disposal of all materials and products, is the key to reducing litter.

According to the author, plastic bags are better for the environment than paper bags, which are more expensive and resource-intensive.

Myth #4: Plastic grocery bags take 1,000 years to decompose in landfills.

Fact: Virtually nothing—not paper, food, plastic or even compostable or bio degradable products—decompose in today's landfills, because they are actually designed to be as stable and dry as possible. Research by William Rathje, who runs the Garbage Project, has shown that when excavated from a landfill, newspapers from the 1960s can be intact and readable.

Myth #5: Plastic bags feed America's addiction to oil.

Fact: Plastic bags are extraordinarily energy-efficient to manufacture. Less than .05% of a barrel of oil goes into making all the plastic bags used in the US while 93%–95% of every barrel of crude oil is burned for fuel and heating purposes. Although they are made from natural gas or oil, plastic bags actually consume less fossil fuels during their lifetime than do compostable plastic and paper bags.

Myth #6: Compostable bags can degrade in backyard composts.

Fact: In order to break down, compostable bags must be sent to an industrial composting facility, not backyard piles or municipal composting centers. There are very few of these facilities in the U.S. and

COUNTERTHINK

FACT: SAN FRANCISCO BANNED PLASTIC BAGS, BUT NOT THE TOXIC FOOD PRODUCTS CARRIED IN THEM.   WWW.HONESTFOODGUIDE.ORG

Courtesy of NaturalNews.com.

where these facilities are not available, compostable bags will sit in landfills because they can't be recycled.

Myth #7: For people who live near water, paper bags are the environmentally friendly choice to protect marine wildlife.

Fact: Since paper bag production has more negative environmental impacts related to air emissions, water emissions and solid waste than plastic grocery bags, they're not a solution. Recycling and proper disposal of all products would make sure that any threat to the environment, including wildlife, would be reduced.

FAST FACT

The Competitive Enterprise Institute states that plastic bags produce 60 percent less greenhouse gases than paper bags.

Myth #8: Low recycling rates for plastic bags prove recycling them doesn't work.

Fact: Recycling does work. The problem is not everyone knows that plastic grocery bags are 100% recyclable and not everyone has access to plastic bag recycling in their community. A national at-store plastic bag recycling program would bring the recycling solution to everyone and increase rates. One Southern supermarket chain has such a program, and recycles more than 20% of the volume of plastic bags that it provides to customers.

Myth #9: Recycling plastic bags is too expensive.

Fact: The price of *not* recycling them is high. Recycling can help save resources and minimize the amount of waste going to landfills. Also, recycling helps reduce litter, as bags are contained and stored. It's worth noting that it takes 91% less energy to recycle a pound of plastic than it takes to recycle a pound of paper.

Myth #10: There's no demand for recycled plastic.

Fact: Today there is a growing market for recycled plastic that didn't exist 15 years ago. It's also cheaper now to use recycled plastic than to obtain new materials, increasing potential for more recycling of used plastic bags. Recycled plastic grocery and shopping bags are currently being made into new consumer products such as clean new plastic shopping bags, outdoor decking and railing products.

Chapter 2

Is Recycling Effective?

A paper recycling plant processes hundreds of tons of paper a day.

Recycling Is Effective

Tom Zeller Jr.

"Recycling ... not only conserves natural resources and reduces the amount of waste that must be burned or buried, it also reduces pollution and the demand for energy."

In the following viewpoint Tom Zeller Jr. weighs the pros and cons of recycling and concludes that recycling makes environmental and economic sense. While he acknowledges that recycling is an expensive and energy-consuming endeavor, the net cost of recycling is less than that of making new products. Many cities have found ways to reduce recycling costs, and even energy spent recycling old products is less than energy spent creating new products, according to Zeller. Furthermore, because new products increase the amount of packaging that gets thrown out, recycling is a good way to reduce the total amount of garbage that is piling up across the globe. Zeller concludes that recycling is energy- and cost-efficient, and he supports laws that require product manufacturers and retailers to share the cost of recycling.

Zeller is an editor at *National Geographic* magazine, an official journal of the National Geographic Society, from which this viewpoint is taken.

1. What are at least three "tree costs" incurred during a product's life span, according to the author?
2. In what percent of cases did recycling prove better than burying or burning waste?
3. According to Zeller, what percent of lead-acid batteries get recycled in the United States?

D oes it make sense to recycle? The short answer is: Yes.
True, some critics wonder whether mandatory programs are a net benefit, since they can require more trucks consuming energy and belching carbon dioxide into the atmosphere.

"You don't want a large truck carrying around just a few bottles," concedes Matthew Hale, director of EPA's [Environmental Protection Agency] Office of Solid Waste. But, he notes, most cities are getting better at reducing the environmental costs of recycling. (They're also working to reduce the economic costs. Many recycling programs still cost more to run than they bring in when they sell the recyclable materials back to manufacturers.)

Consider the true cost of a product over its entire life—from harvesting the raw materials to creating, consuming, and disposing of it—and the scale tips dramatically in recycling's favor. Every shrink-wrapped toy or tool or medical device we buy bears the stamp of its energy-intensive history: mountains of ore that have been mined (bauxite, say, for aluminum cans), coal plants and oil refineries, railcars, assembly lines. A product's true cost includes greenhouse gases emitted in its creation as well as use, and pollutants that cause acid rain, smog, and fouled waterways.

Recycling Is Good for the Environment

Recycling—substituting scrap for virgin materials—not only conserves natural resources and reduces the amount of waste that must be burned or buried, it also reduces pollution and the demand for energy. "You get tremendous Btu [British thermal unit, a measurement of energy] savings," Hale says.

How Are Items Selected for Recycling?

Two main sorting methods are used to isolate recyclable materials: eddy-current separating and spectroscopic sorting.

Eddy-current Separator

1. A stream of waste material moves along a conveyor belt.

3. A secondary magnetic field is induced in metallic items, and magnetic repulsion pushes them clear of the waste stream.

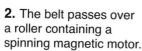

2. The belt passes over a roller containing a spinning magnetic motor.

Spectroscopic Sorter

1. A stream of waste material travels along a conveyor belt and passes under a camera.

2. Each type of material reflects a unique combination of wavelengths in the infrared spectrum and can thus be identified.

3. By firing a jet of air, it is then possible to pick out some items from the waste stream.

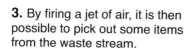

Taken from: Economist.com.

In an international study published last year [2007] by the Waste & Resources Action Programme, a British group, researchers compared more than 180 municipal waste management systems. Recycling proved better for the environment than burying or burning waste in 83 percent of the cases.

It makes sense to reuse products, of course, and to reduce consumption altogether, as well as to improve initial product design. But given the rising mounds of waste worldwide, it also makes sense to recycle.

The United States Is Developing Recycling Infrastructures

What gets recycled in the U.S.[?] It depends on the markets. Whether or not a particular material is recycled depends on a number of factors, but the most fundamental question is this: Is there a market for it? Markets for some materials, like car batteries, are highly developed and efficient—not least because strict regulations govern their disposal—and a mature recycling infrastructure has grown up as a result. About 90 percent of all lead-acid batteries are recycled, according to the EPA. Steel recycling, too, has been around for decades, while formalized recycling of yard trimmings has not. Despite the explosive growth of plastics—particularly for use in beverage containers—that industry has been slow to develop recycling infrastructure, with most plastic still going to incinerators or landfills.

Recycling Is Everyone's Responsibility

Higher hygiene standards, smaller households, intense brand marketing, and the rise of ready-made meals have all contributed to an increase in packaging waste, but international trade may be the biggest factor.

FAST FACT

A 2007 Harris poll found that 77 percent of Americans recycle in their homes.

Even simple items like bottles of water now routinely crisscross the globe, meaning that thirst for a few swallows of "product" can generate not just plastic bottles, but also a large amount of other packaging debris—from wrapping film to bin liners to shipping crates.

So far, Europe has led the world in recycling packaging materials—principally through the Packaging and Packaging Waste Directive of 1994. The EU [European Union] directive calls for manufacturers, retailers, and others in the product chain to share the recycling burden.

The author thinks that recycling materials requires a mature recycling infrastructure like the ones developed for recycling car batteries and their highly toxic materials.

With the exception of hazardous wastes, the United States has been slower to embrace the concept of "extended producer responsibility," as the idea is known, according to Bill Sheehan, director of the Product Policy Institute, a nonprofit research organization in Athens, Georgia. Some municipalities, however, are starting to demand that businesses help cover the costs of recycling.

"Otherwise," Sheehan says, we are "just stimulating the production of more stuff."

EVALUATING THE AUTHOR'S ARGUMENTS:

In the viewpoint you just read, the author suggests that businesses should start paying for some of the recycling costs of their products. What do you think? Is requiring businesses to pay for part of the recycling costs a good idea? Why or why not? Explain your position.

Recycling Is Ineffective

Per Bylund

"Imagine a whole population spending time and money cleaning their garbage and driving it around the neighborhood rather than working or investing in a productive market!"

In the following viewpoint author Per Bylund argues that recycling is inefficient. He claims that people are forced to sort recyclable materials and then have to go out of their way to make sure the materials are disposed of properly. The cost of wasted time from people having to drive the recyclables to trash collection centers, Bylund contends, are not factored into the costs of recycling. Furthermore, the auto emissions from so many people driving to dispose of their garbage is another environmental cost. Bylund refers to a current problem in Stockholm, Sweden, to illustrate another cost of recycling: Trash piled up at collection centers are attracting rats, thus increasing the risk of disease. Yet another problem is that the government forces people to recycle, and in Bylund's opinion this is inappropriate—the government should not have to force its citizens to do anything that is worth doing. For these reasons, Bylund concludes that recycling programs are ineffective.

Per Bylund is an anarchist and libertarian writer and thinker. He writes regularly for the Ludwig von Mises Institute, a research and educational center of liberalism that published this viewpoint.

Per Bylund, "The Recycling Myth," Ludwig von Mises Institute, February 4, 2008. Reproduced by permission.

AS YOU READ, CONSIDER THE FOLLOWING QUESTIONS:
1. What does the term "coercive environmentalism" mean in the context of the viewpoint?
2. Which items does the author say need to be cleaned before throwing away?
3. According to Bylund, what is not factored in by government authorities and researchers when measuring the energy and costs of recycling?

As a Swede I get to hear a lot of the myths of how wonderful a country Sweden supposedly is—the "prosperous socialism" it stands for, a role model for the rest of the world. For instance, quite a few friends from around the world have commended me on Swedish recycling policies and the Swedish government's take on coercive environmentalism.

The way it has been presented to me, Sweden has succeeded with what most other governments at best dream about: creating an efficient and profitable national system for saving the environment through large-scale recycling. And the people are all in on it! Everybody's recycling.

Mandatory Recycling Is Wrong

The latter is actually true: everybody *is* recycling. But that is the result of government force, not a voluntary choice. The state's monopolist garbage-collection "service" no longer accepts garbage: they will only collect leftovers and other biodegradables. Any other kind of garbage that accidentally finds its way to your garbage bin can result in a nice little fine (it really isn't that little) and the whole neighborhood could face increased garbage collection rates (i.e., *even larger* increases than usual—they tend to increase annually or biannually anyway).

So what do you do with your waste? Most homes have a number of trash bins for different kinds of trash: batteries in one; biodegradables in one; wood in one; colored glass in one, other glass in another; aluminum in one, other metals in another; newspapers in one, hard paper in another, and paper that doesn't fit these two categories in a third; and plastic of all sorts in another collection of bins. The materials generally have to be cleaned before thrown away—milk cartons with milk in them cannot be recycled just as metal cans cannot have too much of the paper labels left.

The people of Sweden are thus forced to clean their trash before carefully separating different kinds of materials. This is the future, they say, and it is supposedly good for the environment. (What about the economy?) . . .

Consumers Do Most of the Recycling Work

But the real question here . . . is: does this recycling structure *work?* The answer is that, from a government point of view, while it can probably be thought of as working, from an environmental point of view, the answer is definitely "no."

The structure works the way all centrally planned structures work: it increases and centralizes power while the attempted (expected) results do not materialize. In this case, the structure works: people do sort their trash in different bins—they have no choice. Also, government garbage collection companies do not have to do as much work while getting paid more than ever before. People are annoyed, but do not really react. Swedes generally complain a lot (about *everything*), but they do not resist; they are used to being pushed around by powerful government and have tolerated this fate ever since 1523 [when modern Sweden was founded].

This coercive recycling structure is set up in layers, where the consumer ("producer" of waste) gets to do most of the work of sorting, cleaning, and transporting the trash to collection centers. Government-appointed companies then empty the containers and transport the materials to regional centers where the trash is prepared for recycling. And then everything is transported to centralized recycling plants where the materials are prepared for reuse or burning. Finally what is left of the materials is sold to companies and individuals at subsidized prices so that they can make "environmentally friendly" choices.

What is interesting about this Soviet-style planned recycling is that it is officially profitable. It is supposed to be resource efficient, since recycling of the materials is less energy-consuming than, for instance, mining or the production of paper from wood. It is also economically

The people of Sweden are forced to clean their trash before separating and recycling different materials. Critics say this type of recycling program hurts the economy.

profitable, since the government actually generates revenues from selling recycled materials and products made in the recycling process. The final recycling process costs less than is earned from selling the recycled products.

Recycling Is Not Efficient

However, this is common *government* logic: it is "energy saving" simply because government does not count the time and energy used by *nine million people* cleaning and sorting their trash. Government authorities and researchers have reached the conclusion that the cost of (a) the water and electricity used for cleaning household trash, (b) transportation from trash collection centers, and (c) the final recycling process is actually less than would be necessary to produce these materials from scratch. Of course, they don't count the literally millions of times people drive to the recycling centers to empty their trash bins; neither do they count, for instance, energy and costs for the extra housing space required for a dozen extra trash bins in every home.

Economically, Swedish recycling is a disaster. Imagine a whole population spending time and money cleaning their garbage and

United States Beverage Container Recycling, 1990–2005

Recycling rates have declined since the early 1990s, despite the fact that the population served by curbside recycling programs has almost quadrupled.

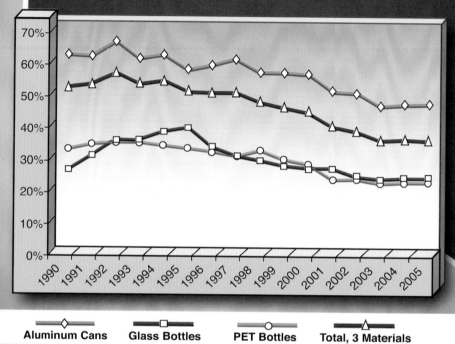

Aluminum Cans — ◇   **Glass Bottles** — □   **PET Bottles** — ○   **Total, 3 Materials** — △

Taken from: Data derived from Aluminum Association, U.S. Commerce Dept., U.S. EPA Office of Solid Waste, American Plastics Council, National Association of PET Container Resources, and Beverage Marketing Corporation.

driving it around the neighborhood rather than working or investing in a productive market! According to the movement's books, more money flows in than flows out; therefore recycling is profitable. But this ignores the costs of coercion.

Recycling Breeds Vermin and Disease

The government bookkeepers also take advantage of the cost cuts they have been able to realize through centralizing the garbage collection system. These "cuts," however, are mostly cuts in service, whereas rates for consumers have been increased. A recent problem with the garbage-collection centers is that the containers aren't emptied very often (a typical example of government "savings") and thus remain full, which means that people's garbage piles up next to the overflowing containers while the government contractors sit idle: they are only paid to empty the containers on schedule, not to pick up the trash sitting next to these containers. The result? Disease and rats. Newspapers have been reporting on a "rat invasion" in Stockholm and in other Swedish cities in recent years.

If we consider the costs in monetary terms, in terms of wasted time, and in terms of increased emissions from automobiles, this is hardly environmentally friendly. Adding the annoyance and the increased risk for disease, Swedish recycling is at least as disastrous as any other government scheme. . . .

Please enlighten me, wherein lies the so-often-acclaimed *success* of this system?

EVALUATING THE AUTHORS' ARGUMENTS:

The author of the previous viewpoint argues that recycling reduces energy use and pollution. How do you think Bylund might respond to that claim? Support your answer with evidence from the texts you have read.

Recycling Is Environmentally Friendly

Economist

"If done right, there is no doubt that recycling saves energy and raw materials, and reduces pollution."

This viewpoint is taken from the *Economist*, a British paper that reports on politics, science and technology, cultural trends, and business. The anonymous author argues that recycling is environmentally friendly and claims that recycling reduces air pollution because it causes less waste to be burned in incinerators and reduces the amount that must be stored in landfills (which give off methane and other toxic emissions). Recycling also conserves natural resources because it makes products out of already existing materials instead of mining for new or raw materials. In addition, the author reports that new recycling technologies require less human labor and less transport than in the past, making the process more efficient than ever. Also, more companies are packaging their products in recycled materials, which further reduces carbon dioxide emissions and garbage. For all of these reasons, the author concludes that recycling is environmentally friendly and supports global efforts to boost recycling efforts.

AS YOU READ, CONSIDER THE FOLLOWING QUESTIONS:
1. According to the author, what percentage of energy consumption is reduced when aluminum, plastic, steel, paper, and glass are recycled?
2. Explain the concept of "single stream" collection, as described by the author.
3. What does the Sustainable Packaging Coalition advocate, as described by the author?

It is an awful lot of rubbish. Since 1960 the amount of municipal waste being collected in America has nearly tripled, reaching 245m tonnes in 2005. According to European Union statistics, the amount of municipal waste produced in western Europe increased by 23% between 1995 and 2003, to reach 577kg per person. (So much for the plan to reduce waste per person to 300kg by 2000.) As the volume of waste has increased, so have recycling efforts. In 1980 America recycled only 9.6% of its municipal rubbish; today the rate stands at 32%. A similar trend can be seen in Europe, where some countries, such as Austria and the Netherlands, now recycle 60% or more of their municipal waste. Britain's recycling rate, at 27%, is low, but it is improving fast, having nearly doubled in the past three years.

Recycling Benefits the Environment

Even so, when a city introduces a kerbside recycling programme, the sight of all those recycling lorries trundling around can raise doubts about whether the collection and transportation of waste materials requires more energy than it saves. "We are constantly being asked: Is recycling worth doing on environmental grounds?" says Julian Parfitt, principal analyst at Waste & Resources Action Programme (WRAP), a non-profit British company that encourages recycling and develops markets for recycled materials.

Studies that look at the entire life cycle of a particular material can shed light on this question in a particular case, but WRAP decided to take a broader look. It asked the Technical University of Denmark and the Danish Topic Centre on Waste to conduct a review of 55 life-cycle analyses, all of which were selected because of their rigorous methodology. The researchers then looked at more than 200 scenarios, comparing the impact of recycling with that of burying or burning particular types of waste material. They found that in 83% of all scenarios that included recycling, it was indeed better for the environment.

There Are Many Benefits to Recycling

Based on this study, WRAP calculated that Britain's recycling efforts reduce its carbon-dioxide emissions by 10m–15m tonnes per year. That is equivalent to a 10% reduction in Britain's annual carbon-dioxide emissions from transport, or roughly equivalent to taking 3.5m cars off the roads. Similarly, America's Environmental Protection Agency estimates that recycling reduced the country's carbon emissions by 49m tonnes in 2005.

Recycling has many other benefits, too. It conserves natural resources. It also reduces the amount of waste that is buried or burnt, hardly ideal ways to get rid of the stuff. (Landfills take up valuable space and emit methane, a potent greenhouse gas; and although incinerators are not as polluting as they once were, they still produce noxious emissions, so people dislike having them around.) But perhaps the most valuable benefit of recycling is the saving in energy and the reduction in greenhouse gases and pollution that result when scrap materials are substituted for virgin feedstock. "If you can use recycled materials, you don't have to mine ores, cut trees and drill for oil as much," says Jeffrey Morris of Sound Resource Management, a consulting firm based in Olympia, Washington.

Extracting metals from ore, in particular, is extremely energy-intensive. Recycling aluminium, for example, can reduce energy consumption by as much as 95%. Savings for other materials are lower but still substantial: about 70% for plastics, 60% for steel, 40% for paper and 30% for glass. Recycling also reduces emissions of pollutants that can cause smog, acid rain and the contamination of waterways. . . .

New Recycling Technologies Require Less Human Labor

Originally kerbside programmes asked people to put paper, glass and cans into separate bins. But now the trend is toward co-mingled or "single stream" collection. About 700 of America's 10,000 kerbside

Energy Savings per Ton Recycled*

* Assumes recycled materials would otherwise have been landfilled

When products are made from recycled materials rather than raw materials, energy is saved.

Material	Million Btu/ton
Textbooks	0.7
Magazines/Third-Class Mail	1.1
Glass	2.7
Office Paper	10.2
Phonebooks	11.9
Corrugated Cardboard	15.7
Newspaper	16.9
Steel Cans	20.5
Personal Computers	44.0
Copper Wire	83.1
Carpet	106.1
Aluminum Cans	206.9

Taken from: Environmental Protection Agency.

programmes now use this approach, says Kate Krebs, executive director of America's National Recycling Coalition. But the switch can make people suspicious: if there is no longer any need to separate different materials, people may conclude that the waste is simply being buried or burned. In fact, the switch towards single-stream collection is being driven by new technologies that can identify and sort the various materials with little or no human intervention. Single-stream collection makes it more convenient for householders to recycle, and means that more materials are diverted from the waste stream.

San Francisco, which changed from multi to single-stream collection a few years ago, now boasts a recycling rate of 69%—one of the highest in America. With the exception of garden and food waste, all the city's kerbside recyclables are sorted in a 200,000-square-foot facility that combines machines with the manpower of 155 employees. The $38m plant, next to the San Francisco Bay, opened in 2003. Operated by Norcal Waste Systems, it processes an average of 750 tons of paper, plastic, glass and metals a day. . . .

Recycling Encourages New Packaging Designs

One of the biggest barriers to more efficient recycling is that most products were not designed with recycling in mind. Remedying this problem may require a complete rethinking of industrial processes, says William McDonough, an architect and the co-author of a book pub-

Denmark burns waste materials in an incinerator plant that produces energy for heating the district and is better for the environment.

lished in 2002 called "Cradle to Cradle: Remaking the Way We Make Things". Along with Michael Braungart, his fellow author and a chemist, he lays out a vision for establishing "closed-loop" cycles where there is no waste. Recycling should be taken into account at the design stage, they argue, and all materials should either be able to return to the soil safely or be recycled indefinitely. This may sound like wishful thinking, but Mr McDonough has a good pedigree. Over the years he has worked with companies including Ford and Google.

An outgrowth of "Cradle to Cradle" is the Sustainable Packaging Coalition, a non-profit working group that has developed guidelines that look beyond the traditional benchmarks of packaging design to emphasise the use of renewable, recycled and non-toxic source materials, among other things. Founded in 2003 with just nine members, the group now boasts nearly 100 members, including Target, Starbucks and Estée Lauder, some of which have already begun to change the design of their packaging.

Sustainable packaging not only benefits the environment but can also cut costs. Last year Wal-Mart, the world's biggest retailer, announced that it wanted to reduce the amount of packaging it uses by 5% by 2013, which could save the company as much as $3.4 billion and reduce carbon-dioxide emissions by 667,000 tonnes. As well as trying to reduce the amount of packaging, Wal-Mart also wants to recycle more of it. Two years ago the company began to use an unusual process, called the "sandwich bale", to collect waste material at its stores and distribution centres for recycling. It involves putting a layer of cardboard at the bottom of a rubbish compactor before filling it with waste material, and then putting another layer of cardboard on top. The compactor then produces a "sandwich" which is easier to handle and transport, says Jeff Ashby of Rocky Mountain Recycling, who invented the process for Wal-Mart. As well as avoiding disposal costs for materials it previously sent to landfill, the company now makes money by selling waste at market prices.

Recycling Reduces Waste

Evidently there is plenty of scope for further innovation in recycling. New ideas and approaches will be needed, since many communities and organisations have set high targets for recycling. Europe's packaging directive requires member states to recycle 60% of their glass and paper, 50% of metals and 22.5% of plastic packaging by the end of 2008. Earlier this year the European Parliament voted to increase recycling rates by 2020 to 50% of municipal waste and 70% of industrial waste. Recycling rates can be boosted by charging households and businesses more if they produce more rubbish, and by reducing the frequency of rubbish collections while increasing that of recycling collections.

Meanwhile a number of cities and firms (including Wal-Mart, Toyota and Nike) have adopted zero-waste targets. This may be unrealistic but Matt Hale, director of the office of solid waste at America's Environmental Protection Agency, says it is a worthy goal and can help companies think about better ways to manage materials. It forces people to look at the entire life-cycle of a product, says Dr Hale, and ask questions: Can you reduce the amount of material to begin with? Can you design the product to make recycling easier?

If done right, there is no doubt that recycling saves energy and raw materials, and reduces pollution. But as well as trying to recycle more, it is also important to try to recycle better. As technologies and materials evolve, there is room for improvement and cause for optimism. In the end, says Ms Krebs, "waste is really a design flaw."

EVALUATING THE AUTHOR'S ARGUMENTS:

The author of this viewpoint quotes from several sources to support the points made in the essay. Make a list of all the people quoted, including their credentials and the nature of their comments. Then, analyze the sources. Are they credible? Are they well qualified to speak on this subject?

Recycling Is Not Environmentally Friendly

Daniel K. Benjamin

"Recycling merely changes the nature of pollution— sometimes decreasing it, and sometimes increasing it."

In the following viewpoint author Daniel K. Benjamin argues that recycling does not help conserve natural resources or protect the environment. He believes that recycling programs are an overreaction to myths the public has been fed about a so-called garbage crisis. Benjamin contends that no such crisis exists: In his opinion, there is enough space to hold all of America's garbage, landfills do not produce dangerous gases, and natural resources are not being depleted. Furthermore, he suggests that recycling may produce as much pollution as primary manufacturing and curbside recycling programs because more vehicles are required to transport the trash to and from recycling centers. He points out that landfills have more capacity for trash than ever before and that harmful gases emitted by landfills are not due to household waste but by illegally dumped industrial waste. Benjamin concludes there are enough resources to meet the world's demand for products and that recycling is an unnecessary activity that uses more resources than it saves.

Daniel K. Benjamin, "The Eight Myths of Recycling," *American Enterprise,* January/February, 2004. Reproduced with permission of *The American Enterprise,* a national magazine of Politics, Business, and Culture (TAEmag.com).

Benjamin is a professor at Clemson University and a senior fellow at PERC, the Property and Environment Research Center.

AS YOU READ, CONSIDER THE FOLLOWING QUESTIONS:
1. What evidence does the author provide to argue that Americans are not squandering natural resources?
2. How many trucks did the city of Los Angeles add to its fleet to handle the curbside recycling program, according to the author?
3. According to Benjamin, what percent more does curbside recycling cost than throwing an item away?

The modern era of the recycling craze can be traced to 1987, when the garbage barge *Mobro 4000* had to spend two months touring the Atlantic and the Gulf of Mexico before it found a home for its load. The Environmental Defense Fund, the National Solid Waste Management Association (whose members were anxious to line up new customers for their expanding landfill capacity), the press, and finally the Environmental Protection Agency [EPA], spun the story of a garbage crisis out of control. By 1995, the majority of Americans thought trash was our number one environmental problem—with 77 percent reporting that increased recycling of household rubbish was the solution. Yet these claims and fears were based on errors and misinformation, which I have compiled into the Eight Great Myths of Recycling.

Myth 1: Our Garbage Will Bury Us

Fact: Even though the United States is larger, more affluent, and producing more garbage, it now has more landfill capacity than ever before. The erroneous opposite impression comes from old studies that counted the number of landfills (which has declined) rather than landfill capacity (which has grown). There are a few places, like New Jersey, where capacity has shrunk. But the uneven distribution of landfill space is no more important than the uneven distribution of automobile manufacturing. Perhaps the most important fact is this: If we permitted our rubbish to grow to the height of New York City's famous Fresh Kills landfill (225 feet), a site only about 10 miles on a side could hold all of America's garbage for the next century.

Myth 2: Our Garbage Will Poison Us

Fact: Almost anything can pose a theoretical threat, but evidence of actual harm from landfills is almost non-existent, as the Environmental Protection Agency itself acknowledges. The EPA has concluded that landfills constructed according to agency regulations can be expected to cause a total of 5.7 cancer-related deaths over the next 300 years. It isn't household waste, but improperly or illegally dumped industrial wastes that can be harmful. Household recycling programs have no effect on those wastes, a fact ignored by messianic proponents of recycling.

Myth 3: Our Packaging Is Immoral

Fact: Many people argue that the best way to "save landfill space" is to reduce the amount of packaging Americans use, via mandatory controls. But packaging can actually reduce total garbage produced and total resources used. The average American family generates fully one third less trash than does the average Mexican household. The reason is that our intensive use of packaging yields less spoilage and breakage, thereby saving resources, and producing, on balance, less total rubbish. Careful packaging also reduces food poisoning and other health problems.

Over the past 25 years, market incentives have already reduced the weights of individual packages by 30 to 70 percent. An average aluminum can weighed nearly 21 grams in 1972; in 2002, that same can weighs in at under 14 grams. A plastic grocery sack was 2.3 mils thick in 1976; by 2001, it was a mere 0.7 mils.

By contrast, the environmentally sensitive *New York Times* has been growing. A year's worth of the newspaper now weighs 520 pounds and occupies more than 40 cubic feet in a landfill. This is equivalent in weight to 17,180 aluminum cans—nearly a century's worth of beer and soft drink consumption by one person. Clearly, people anxious to heal Mother Earth must forego the *Times*!

Myth 4: We Must Achieve "Trash Independence"

Fact: Garbage has become an inter-state business, with 47 states exporting the stuff and 45 importing it. Environmentalists contend that each state should dispose within its borders all the trash produced within its borders. But why? Transporting garbage across an arbitrary legal boundary has no effect on the environmental impact of the disposal of that material. Moving a ton of trash is no more hazardous than moving a ton of any other commodity.

Myth 5: We're Squandering Irreplaceable Resources

Fact: Thanks to numerous innovations, we now produce about twice as much output per unit of energy as we did 50 years ago, and five times as much as we did 200 years ago. Automobiles use only half as much metal as in 1970, and one optical fiber carries the same number of calls as 625 copper wires did 20 years ago. Bridges are built with less steel, because steel is stronger and engineering is improved. Automobile and truck engines consume less fuel per unit of work performed, and produce fewer emissions. . . .

Myth 6: Recycling Always Protects the Environment

Fact: Recycling is a manufacturing process, and therefore it too has environmental impact. The U.S. Office of Technology Assessment says that it is "not clear whether secondary manufacturing [i.e., recycling] produces less pollution per ton of material processed than primary manufacturing." Recycling merely changes the nature of pollution—sometimes decreasing it, and sometimes increasing it.

This effect is particularly apparent in the case of curbside recycling, which is mandated or strongly encouraged by governments in many communities around the country. Curbside recycling requires that more trucks be used to collect the same amount of waste materials. Instead of one truck picking up 40 pounds of garbage, one will pick up four pounds of recyclables and a second will collect 36 pounds of rubbish.

> **FAST FACT**
>
> A study by the Environmental Protection Agency found that recycled paper processing creates higher levels of toxic substances than virgin paper processing.

Los Angeles has estimated that due to curbside recycling, its fleet of trucks is twice as large as it otherwise would be—800 vs. 400 trucks. This means more iron ore and coal mining, more steel and rubber

The 1987 Mobro *garbage barge (above) incident is credited by the author as the beginning of the modern era of recycling. The* Mobro *wandered the oceans for two months in search of disposal.*

manufacturing, more petroleum extracted and refined for fuel—and of course all that extra air pollution in the Los Angeles basin as the 400 added trucks cruise the streets.

Myth 7: Recycling Saves Resources

Fact: Using less of one resource usually means using more of another. Curbside recycling is substantially more costly and uses far more resources than a program in which disposal is combined with a voluntary drop-off/buy-back option. The reason: Curbside recycling of household rubbish uses huge amounts of capital and labor per pound of material recycled. Overall, curbside recycling costs between 35 and 55 percent more than simply disposing of the item. It typically wastes resources.

In the ordinary course of daily living, we already reuse most higher value items. The only things that intentionally end up in the trash are both low in value and costly to reuse or recycle. Yet these are the items that municipal recycling programs are targeting—the very things that consumers have already decided are too worthless or costly to deal with further. All of the profitable, socially productive opportunities for recycling were long ago co-opted by the private sector, because they

Plastic Produced Versus Plastics Recycled

Many more new plastic products are made from raw materials than are recycled. Some say this is because the process of recycling itself wastes energy and resources.

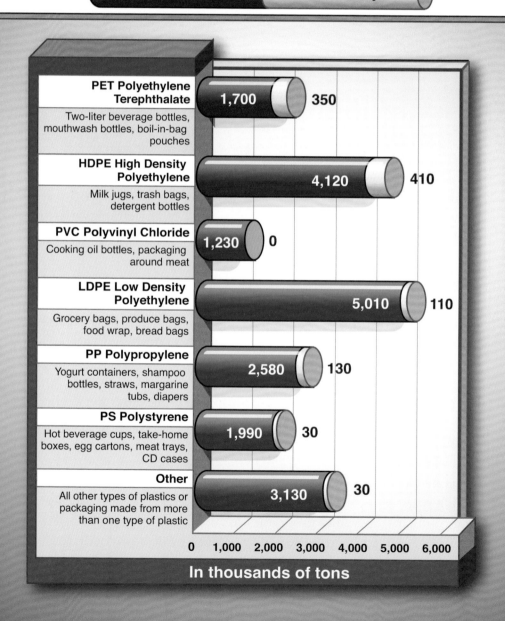

Amount Produced   **Amount Recycled**

PET Polyethylene Terephthalate
Two-liter beverage bottles, mouthwash bottles, boil-in-bag pouches
1,700 — 350

HDPE High Density Polyethylene
Milk jugs, trash bags, detergent bottles
4,120 — 410

PVC Polyvinyl Chloride
Cooking oil bottles, packaging around meat
1,230 — 0

LDPE Low Density Polyethylene
Grocery bags, produce bags, food wrap, bread bags
5,010 — 110

PP Polypropylene
Yogurt containers, shampoo bottles, straws, margarine tubs, diapers
2,580 — 130

PS Polystyrene
Hot beverage cups, take-home boxes, egg cartons, meat trays, CD cases
1,990 — 30

Other
All other types of plastics or packaging made from more than one type of plastic
3,130 — 30

0   1,000   2,000   3,000   4,000   5,000   6,000

In thousands of tons

Taken from: U.S. Department of Energy.

pay back. The bulk of all curbside recycling programs simply waste resources.

Myth 8: Without Forced Mandates, There Wouldn't Be Any Recycling

Fact: Long before state or local governments had even contemplated the word recycling, the makers of steel, aluminum, and thousands of other products were recycling manufacturing scraps. Some operated post-consumer drop-off centers. As for the claim that the private sector promotes premature or excessive disposal, this ignores an enormous body of evidence to the contrary. Firms only survive in the marketplace if they take into account all costs. Fifty years ago, when labor was cheap compared to materials, goods were built to be repaired, so that the expensive materials could be used for a longer period of time. As the price of labor has risen and the cost of materials has fallen, manufacturers have responded by building items to be used until they break, and then discarded. There is no bias against recycling; there is merely a market-driven effort to conserve the most valuable resources. . . .

Except in a few rare cases, the free market is eminently capable of providing both disposal and recycling in an amount and mix that creates the greatest wealth for society. This makes possible the widest and most satisfying range of human endeavors. Simply put, market prices are sufficient to induce the trash-man to come, and to make his burden bearable, and neither he nor we can hope for any better than that.

EVALUATING THE AUTHORS' ARGUMENTS:

To make his argument that recycling is not environmentally friendly, Benjamin explores some of the "hidden" costs of recycling—for example, the energy spent transporting recyclables to and from recycling centers. Make a list of the hidden costs he discusses. Then, for each one, write one sentence saying how you think each author in this chapter would support or refute the claim.

Recycling Conserves Resources

City of Fort Collins, Colorado

"Recycling's true value comes from preventing pollution and saving natural resources and energy, not landfill space."

The following viewpoint was published by the City of Fort Collins Recycling Department. In it, the author contends that recycling conserves natural resources and energy. According to the author, recycling conserves timber, water, and mineral ores. Furthermore, when products are made from recycled sources, less energy is used because the materials are not raw and have already been processed. This conserves not only energy but resources as well. For example, when fewer minerals are processed, less toxic emissions are released into the air and water. In addition to the environmental benefits of recycling, the author argues that recycling helps save money spent on manufacturing and also creates thousands of recycling-related jobs. The author concludes that recycling is successful because it protects the environment, reduces waste and pollution, promotes a sense of community, and creates economic incentives.

"Why Recycling Matters," City of Fort Collins, CO. fcgov.com. Accessed May 7, 2008. Reproduced by permission.

There are numerous reasons why . . . citizens and businesses [should be encouraged] to recycle. They include a broad range of environmental stewardship concerns, as well as practical interest in local economic opportunities and development, including: cost savings, extended landfill lifespans, resource conservation, energy conservation, economic development, pollution prevention, greenhouse gas emissions reductions, and fostering a sense of community involvement and responsibility.

1. Cost Savings

At a basic level that most people can relate to, recycling prevents materials that have economic value from going to waste. We tend to think of the conventional list of commodities, whose trade values are posted on the Chicago stock exchange; steel, aluminum, paper goods, plastics #1 & 2, and glass. But increasingly, other materials are becoming economically attractive to salvagers: clothing fabric, shrink-wrap, grease, and old computers, just to name a few.

Nationally, the Environmental Protection Agency (EPA) estimates about 30% of the waste stream gets diverted from landfill disposal (unfortunately, it's much lower in Colorado), but there is still a lot that is not getting recycled—meaning money and resources that are getting wasted. . . .

Well-run recycling programs cost less to operate than waste collection, landfilling, and incinerations. Loveland [Colorado] has discovered that the municipal garbage utility's costs to recycle are almost $40 per ton less than the cost to landfill trash, while Denver's recycling programs saved about $200,000 in landfill costs in 2004 and brought in nearly $1 million from the sale of recyclables. Unlike many public services, recycling does function within the market economy, and quite successfully.

2. Extend Landfill Lifespans

Recycling's true value comes from preventing pollution and saving natural resources and energy, not landfill space. Still, it's important to note that recycling is largely responsible for averting a landfill crisis in many parts of the country. Recycling and composting diverted nearly 70 million tons of material away from landfills and incinerators in 2000, up from 34 million tons in 1990.

As regulations have become more rigorous, the number of permitted landfills in the United States has dropped by 78% since 1988. New landfills are much larger than in the past, and more controversial to build because few people are willing to live in the vicinity of a mega-landfill.

While the Larimer County landfill currently is expected to last another 15–19 years (or longer, depending on how successful we are at diverting waste), once it does need to be replaced, a new one will cost taxpayers over $17 million to construct.

3. Conserve Resources

Recycling conserves natural resources, such as timber, water and mineral ores. National statistics point to the environmental success of recovery levels for some materials: paper and paperboard 48%; glass 19%; steel 36%; aluminum 21%. (We have not been as successful at recovering others, for example plastics at 5% and textiles at 14%).

Recovered paper currently accounts for 37% of the paper industry's fiber needs. Without recycling, this material would come from trees; every ton of newspaper is the equivalent of 12 trees, and every ton of office paper is the equivalent of 24 trees. When one ton of steel is recycled, 2,500 pounds of iron ore, 1,400 pounds of coal, and 120 pounds of limestone are conserved. Recycling a ton of paper saves 7,000 gallons of water.

Tree farms and reclaimed mines are not ecologically equivalent to natural forests and ecosystems. Recycling prevents natural habitat destruction, loss of biodiversity, and soil erosion associated with logging and mining.

Recycling Can Be Profitable

Unrecycled commodities could save and generate millions, even billions, of dollars if they were recycled.

Material	Nat'l recycling rate	Unrecycled pounds	Value of unrecycled pounds
Aluminum Cans	51.2%	1,446,843,750	$954,916,875
Fiber	50.2%	99,699,203,185	$3,813,494,522
Glass Bottles	22.0%	75,730,909,091	$18,478,342
HDPE Plastic Bottles	24.2%	2,508,980,000	$577,065,400
PET Plastic Bottles	19.6%	3,449,816,326	$931,450,408
Steel Cans	62.0%	801,661,129	$43,089,286
TOTAL		**183,637,413,481**	**$6,338,494,833**

Taken from: City of Fort Collins, Colorado.

It is not an exaggeration to say that recycling helps ease demand for certain resources that are being extracted in emerging nations under war-torn, repressive governments. For example, a mineral called Tantalum—better known as "coltan"—is used to produce capacitors in electronic devices, especially cell phones (from which it can be recycled). Coltan mining is contributing to political tension between Congo and Rwanda, as well as loss of habitat for the threatened Eastern Lowland Gorilla. Smuggled coltan has been implicated as a major source of income for the military occupation of Congo.

4. Conserve Energy

Supplying recycled materials to industry uses less energy than supplying virgin materials that incur extra extraction and transportation

The U.S. recycling industry employs over a million people with an annual payroll of 37 billion dollars. More recycling plants could create even more jobs.

costs. Additional energy savings associated with recycling accrue in the manufacturing process itself, since the materials have already undergone processing. And of course, by saving energy, recycling helps the U.S. reduce its reliance on oil.

Recycling aluminum saves the nation 95% of the energy that would have been needed to make new aluminum from ore: one aluminum can saves enough electricity to light a 100-watt bulb for 3 1/2 hours. It takes 60% less energy to recycle steel than it does to make it from raw materials. Making recycled newspaper saves 40%, recycled plastics 70%, and recycled glass 40%.

The EPA reported that in 2000, recycling resulted in an annual energy savings equal to the amount of energy used in 6 million homes—over 660 trillion BTU's [British thermal units]—and expected that to rise to 900 trillion BTUs in 2005.

5. Create Jobs / Economic Development

Recycling is a big industry, comparable in size to our auto and truck manufacturing industry. In 2000, it employed over 1.1 million people and generated an annual payroll of $37 billion, representing a significant force in the country's economy, job creation and economic development. For comparison, incinerating 10,000 tons of waste creates one job and landfilling 10,000 tons of waste creates six jobs; recycling 10,000 tons of waste creates 36 jobs.

The public sector's investment in local recycling programs pays great dividends by creating private sector jobs. For every job collecting recyclables, there are 26 jobs in processing the materials and manufacturing them into new products.

As an example of how efficiently the salvage market functions, a recycled aluminum beverage can returns to the grocer's shelf as a new, filled can in as few as 60 days after collection. The steel industry recycles nearly 19 billion cans into new products each year, or about 600 cans per second.

6. Prevent Pollution

Manufacturing with recycled materials, with very few exceptions, produces less air and water pollution than manufacturing with virgin materials. It results in a net reduction for ten major categories of air pollutants (such as nitrogen oxide, particulates, and sulfur oxides) and eight major categories of water pollutants.

In the U.S., processing minerals contributes almost half of all reported toxic emissions from industry, sending 1.5 million tons of pollution into the air and water each year. Recycling can significantly reduce these emissions.

Landfills can be major sources of groundwater pollution if watery "leachate" escapes through underlying clay or plastic linings. Leachate from municipal landfills is similar in composition to that of hazardous waste landfills and in fact, 20% of the sites on the Superfund list (the nation's most hazardous sites) are solid waste landfills.

> **FAST FACT**
>
> The organization Recycling International reports that 1.5 million people are employed in the recycling industry worldwide.

Consumer electronics are creating a growing source of pollution, constituting 40% of the lead found in landfills. The National Safety

Council predicts that in the U.S. between as many as 680 million computers will become obsolete within the next few years; in addition to 1 billion pounds of lead, this waste will contain more than 4 billion pounds of plastic, 1.9 million pounds of cadmium, 1.2 million pounds of chromium, and nearly 400,000 pounds of mercury.

7. Reduce Greenhouse Gas Emissions

Methane is a major greenhouse gas that is 20 to 30 times more potent in its global warming effects than carbon dioxide, and municipal solid waste (MSW) landfills are the largest source of human-related methane emissions in the United States, accounting for about 34% of these emissions.

For every 6 tons of recycled container glass used, 1 ton of carbon dioxide, a greenhouse gas, is reduced. Recycling one ton of aluminum is equivalent to not releasing 13 tons of carbon dioxide into the air.

EVALUATING THE AUTHOR'S ARGUMENTS:

In the viewpoint you just read, the author uses facts and examples to show that recycling conserves resources and energy. However, there are no quotations to support this point. If you were to rewrite this article and insert quotations, what authorities might you quote from? Where would you place these quotations to bolster the points made in this article?

Recycling Wastes Resources

Lucas McMillan

"More trucks and more resources are required to handle the massive bulk of recycling, and all of that transportation ultimately does more harm than good."

In the following viewpoint, author Lucas McMillan argues that recycling wastes more resources than it conserves. He explains that an enormous amount of energy is wasted transporting recyclables to and from collection centers, a process which also causes pollution. These outputs negate and even surpass the resources saved by recycling, he says. Making recycling even less necessary is the fact that there is enough space in U.S. landfills to dispose of trash, and McMillan argues that landfills are environmentally sound. For example, McMillan claims that curbside recycling programs cost more than traditional trash disposal does, use twice the number of trucks, and thus require more gas and produce more pollution. For all of these reasons, McMillan concludes that traditional trash collection and disposal is better than recycling.

This viewpoint was published by *Times-Delphic*, a student-run online news source at Drake University, Des Moines, Iowa.

Lucas McMillan, "Recycling's Myth: The 'Three R's' Are Doing More Harm than Good," *Times-Delphic* (Drake University), November 19, 2007. Reproduced by permission.

AS YOU READ, CONSIDER THE FOLLOWING QUESTIONS:
1. How much trash can U.S. landfills accommodate, and how does that factor into the author's argument about recycling?
2. What was the finding of a study by Franklin Associates, as reported by the author?
3. According to McMillan, how much more expensive is curbside recycling than using a landfill?

"Reduce, Reuse, and Recycle."

This simple phrase is taught every day to children all around America, instilled in them from the beginning. The act of recycling plastics, papers, glass and aluminum is widely hailed by both governments and environmental agencies in both America and Europe as a necessary step toward saving planet Earth.

The Benefits of Recycling Are Exaggerated

The European Union has laid down a set of rules that require citizens of the United Kingdom to double their recycling rates by 2008, while many major cities in the United States, such as New York and Seattle, have proposed vast, required, expansions of existing recycling programs.

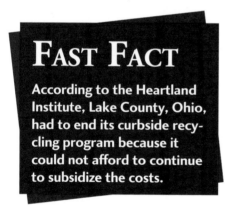

FAST FACT

According to the Heartland Institute, Lake County, Ohio, had to end its curbside recycling program because it could not afford to continue to subsidize the costs.

However, all of these rules and regulations are based in pure myth. Recycling is one of the most unimpeachable environmental movements today, but its benefits are greatly exaggerated and its costs often go completely unreported.

One of the most pervasive myths about recycling is that America is faced with a rising tide of trash and waste, and soon we will be awash in it, completely buried in our own refuse.

Former Vice President Al Gore, for example, once claimed in a speech that we as a nation "are running out of ways to dispose of our waste in a manner that keeps it out of either sight or mind."

Landfills Are Sufficient for Trash Disposal

This is undeniably false. It is true that there are fewer landfills in our country today than there were ten years ago, but their capacity has increased greatly.

According to a study by the Environmental Protection Agency done in 2001, the nation's landfills could accommodate 18 years' worth of trash, an amount 25 percent greater than in the decade preceding it. Recycling is often praised as stemming the massive flood of trash into our landfills; in reality, the total land area required to hold

The author argues that transporting recyclables to processing centers is expensive and unnecessarily wastes resources.

Barriers to Recycling

Americans gave the following answers when asked by pollsters why they did not recycle in their homes. Some southerners said they did not recycle because recycling is not available where they live, while some easterners said they thought recycling was too much effort.

Reason x	Total %	East %	Mid-West %	South %	West %
Not available in our area	15	13	10	20	7
It takes too much effort	12	26	10	12	8
It costs more to recycle where I live	12	5	10	14	12
I don't believe it makes an impact or difference	11	7	8	13	12
I am too busy	6	8	5	6	5
It is too difficult	5	6	9	2	9
No recycling center/drop-off locations near	5	2	4	4	10
No pickup in area	4	8	4	5	3
Live in an apartment/facility that does not provide separate bins	4	3	1	2	13
Don't know how/lack of information	2	–	6	1	*
Not mandatory	2	1	5	*	2
Other	6	8	5	8	5
Not sure	17	14	23	15	15

x = Percentages may not add up to exactly 100% due to rounding.
* = less than 0.5%
– = no response

Taken from: Harris Poll No. 67, "One-Quarter of Americans Do Not Recycle in Their Own Home," July 11, 2007.

all trash produced by the United States for the next century would only be about ten square miles.

Disposing of trash in the conventional way, landfills, is widely reviled. It is often thought of as harmful, toxic and carcinogenic. However, the EPA estimates that there will only be about 5.7 cancer-related deaths caused by landfills in the next 300 years. Landfills are also a reliable source of capital for our country's economy.

Trash is often transported across state lines and traded back and forth, accruing around $4 billion dollars in capital a year.

Recycling Wastes Resources

Proponents of recycling often claim that it "saves resources." They focus on the saving of a particular resource, like the current posters up around Drake stating that "for every ton of recycled newspaper, 17 trees are saved."

That is true, but the long term effects of recycling are detrimental. More trucks and more resources are required to handle the massive bulk of recycling, and all of that transportation ultimately does more harm than good. According to Franklin Associates, an environmental research firm, an extensive recycling program is 35 percent more costly than conventional trash disposal. Curbside recycling pick-ups, the kind most people do, is a staggering 55 percent more costly than a conventional landfill.

Recycling requires twice as many trucks, twice as much gas consumption, and thus twice as much atmospheric pollution. If nothing else, recycling still offers the average citizen a sense of duty and action, like they are really helping to save the world.

"It makes me feel good to be eating at a restaurant or something and to see '100 percent recycled paper' on napkins or placemats," says RHA [Residence Hall Association] recycling activist Liz Pope.

Recycling can help matters to a certain extent, but ultimately it is a counter-productive procedure. Recycling ultimately exacerbates the problems it wishes to solve in the first place.

EVALUATING THE AUTHORS' ARGUMENTS:

At the end of the viewpoint McMillan quotes Liz Pope, who expresses that using recycled products makes her "feel good." What is McMillan's opinion about this "feel good" factor of recycling? What do you think the other authors in this chapter would say about this aspect of the recycling debate?

Chapter 3

What Role Should the Government Play in Garbage and Recycling Efforts?

Local government-run recycling programs can coordinate the efforts of many communities with a centralized plan for waste management.

Viewpoint

1

Recycling Should Be Mandatory

Kathleen Ochshorn

"Though it took a few days to get used to sorting the garbage and we kept the brochure handy in the kitchen, we've come to see the wisdom of the system."

In the following viewpoint Kathleen Ochshorn argues that mandatory recycling laws help reduce waste, lessen environmental impact, create jobs, generate profits, and promote a sense of community. She uses the example of Nova Scotia's recycling laws to show these benefits of mandatory recycling. In that community, residents are required to sort their trash, which keeps nonessential waste out of landfills. Also, trash is picked up once every two weeks, which reduces the gas needed for trash trucks and produces less air pollution. In Ochshorn's opinion, recycling is good for the local economy. She explains that the sale of recyclables brings in profits to the community and also creates jobs in the recycling industry. For all these reasons, Ochshorn concludes that mandatory recycling systems are an effective and profitable way of promoting community environmentalism.

Ochshorn teaches English and writing at the University of Tampa. She is also an editor at the *Tampa Review*.

Kathleen Ochshorn, "A Sort of Trash Therapy," *St. Petersburg Times,* July 29, 2007, p. 1P. Copyright © 2007 *The St. Petersburg Times.* Reproduced by permission of the author.

AS YOU READ, CONSIDER THE FOLLOWING QUESTIONS:
1. What kinds of papers are recyclable, according to the author?
2. According to the author, how much has waste been reduced since Nova Scotia banned recyclable organics from landfills?
3. How much money has been generated from Nova Scotia's recycling program?

W e're in LaHave, Nova Scotia, learning how to talk trash. We've got an eight-page brochure about how to sort it and three bins under the sink. And we don't want our neighbors to think we're ugly Americans who can't deal with their garbage.

Here recycling is mandatory; there are garbage police. And if you don't sort your trash correctly, they simply don't pick it up and you have to root through it again until you get it right. And in LaHave, the pickup is just once every two weeks.

Everyone Should Recycle

In the United States, composting is the province of the odd organic gardener. Here everyone separates out the organics: kitchen scraps, bones, wet paper-like napkins, wrapping paper, boxes, even grass clippings and leaves. Pet detritus and litter appears to be optional: It's organic, but if you have your doubts, they'll let you bag it separately. I've put hair from my brush in the organics, though I'm unsure about its chemical content.

Organics go in a green, lidded bin under the sink and eventually into a green garbage bin outside with an aerated lid, to be collected with everything else. Then gardeners who don't want to keep their own compost pile can buy organic compost from the province for much less than Wal-Mart charges.

Recyclable paper includes newspapers, magazines, corrugated cardboard, and junk mail. But you have to tear the plastic windows out of the envelopes. And people here do just that.

We didn't have trouble keeping organics and paper straight, but things got more complicated when we had to separate true garbage from the recyclables that go in a blue bag. For instance, milk cartons and tin cans are recyclables; whereas chip bags and Styrofoam are true garbage. It does give you a clear sense of what's worst for the planet.

Global Recycling Efforts

The United States recycles less of its paper and glass waste than other industrialized nations.

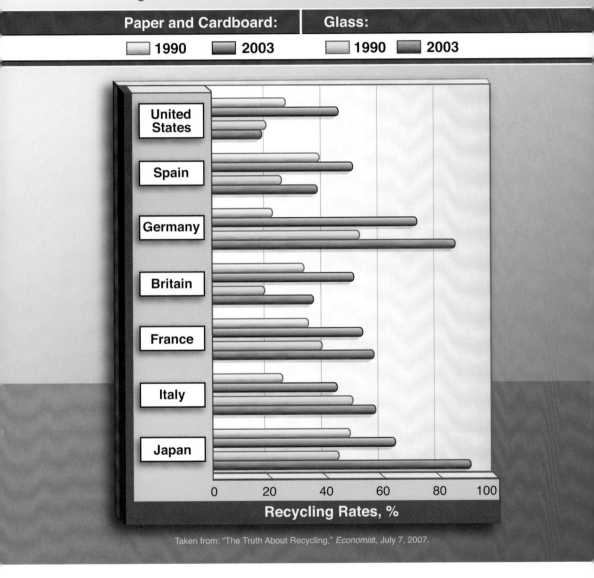

Paper and Cardboard:	Glass:
☐ 1990 ■ 2003	☐ 1990 ■ 2003

Recycling Rates, %

Taken from: "The Truth About Recycling," *Economist*, July 7, 2007.

The night before the scheduled pickup we were peering out the kitchen window, checking our neighbor's pile of bags and bins, hoping we were doing it right. Early the next morning I lugged our stuff out to the curb. When the single brown and tan truck came by, they took it all. No notes from the garbage police!

Though it took a few days to get used to sorting the garbage and we kept the brochure handy in the kitchen, we've come to see the wisdom of the system. A single pickup is simpler for the resident and saves the municipality in truck trips, gas, and air pollution. So I started looking into the history and environmental and financial implications of this system.

Recycling Laws Help Reduce Waste

Bob M. Kenney, a solid waste resource analyst, told me that aversion to organic waste traces back to the days of the bubonic plague, when food scraps began to be carted out of town. But since 1998, Nova Scotia has banned organic material from landfill. Just by separating out organics and recyclables, the province has reduced waste by 50 percent.

Canada is also in the process of banning electronics from landfills and will start charging environmental handling fees on things like computers and televisions at the time of purchase.

Nova Scotians are world leaders in recycling and it began with a grass roots environmental movement. Their waste disposal rate (the trash they must put in landfill) is 45 percent lower than Canada's overall rate and more than 50 percent lower than California's.

And all this is profitable. This province, with a population of 940,000, estimates it comes out $31-million a year ahead. This figure includes the profit from selling recyclables to China, the United States and Canada; the jobs recycling creates; and the reduced environmental impact. And as Kenney pointed out, making things from recycled material takes less energy. Most importantly, the public has embraced the process and takes pride in the environmental effort.

FAST FACT

According to the Environmental Protection Agency, there are approximately 8,660 curbside recycling programs in the United States.

Recycling Is a Responsible Thing to Do

I started wondering if the culture up here predisposes people to take ownership of these issues. They've seen a decline in the logging and fishing industries due to exploitation. It's not an affluent region and

Signs for separate recyclable items are displayed above garbage bins in Nova Scotia, Canada.

second-hand clothiers like Guy Frenchy's and Bargain Bob's abound. Junk shops are also common and there's joy in bargain hunting. Generally, it's a frugal, waste-not-want-not place.

When I spoke to Sally Steele, Lunenburg waste reduction coordinator, she added that the severity of the climate here helps people work closely together, gathering wood or sharing tools, for example. She heads up an educational program that introduces "green teams" of students who take the recycling message to other students. In schools, trash is sorted in lunchrooms and classrooms. The recycling motto here is "Reduce Reuse Recycle."

So would such a streamlined and aggressive recycling system work in Florida [or other places in the United States]? It would certainly reduce the times we put garbage out, perhaps to once a week. It would also make us take more ownership over our waste, over the environmental impact of our lives. Maybe it would even accomplish the goal they've set up here: to make consumers consider avoiding overly packaged items and avoiding unnecessary purchases altogether. After all, how much stuff do we really need?

Viewpoint

2

Recycling Should Not Be Mandatory

Michael D. Shaw

"Recycling surely has its place, and its role is growing, but it is not the holy grail."

In the following viewpoint author Michael D. Shaw argues that recycling should not be required by law. Shaw believes that recycling efforts are more of a trend than a science-based solution for environmental problems. He contends that although some recycling programs yield good end-products, there are enough renewable resources and enough space in landfills to avoid recycling. Shaw points out manufacturers are finding creative ways to turn recycled materials into profitable products, such as milk jugs used for plastic lumber, without mandated recycling programs in place. In Shaw's opinion, Americans have overly glorified the role of recycling as the only way waste management programs can be run successfully. Shaw concludes that since voluntary recycling is sufficient, there is no need to require it by law.

Shaw is executive vice president and director of marketing for Interscan Corporation, a manufacturer of toxic gas detection instrumentation. He is also a contributing columnist for *HealthNewsDigest.com*, which covers health, science, and environmental news.

Michael D. Shaw, "Got Waste? The Debate over Recycling," HealthNewsDigest.com, May 23, 2005. Reproduced by permission of the author.

AS YOU READ, CONSIDER THE FOLLOWING QUESTIONS:
1. According to the author, recycling is like what other fads?
2. For what purpose does Shaw say many trees are specifically grown?
3. Describe the event the author says began the recycling craze. How does it support his argument?

J ust how much of what we do every day is based on popular fads or fashion—as opposed to cold, scientific reason? More than most of us would want to admit, I'm afraid.

Recycling Is a Fad

The global cooling scare of the 1970's morphed into today's global warming. Breast feeding, presumably a proven commodity over human and mammalian history for millions of years, fell out of favor in the 1950's as not being "modern," and even gross. How many baby boomers were raised on the notion that having meat for at least all three meals, seven days a week, was the only way to build strong American bodies? And, who wasn't indoctrinated into the feel-good notion, raised to a religious precept by some, that recycling is the cornerstone of any waste management program, and must be practiced by all people all the time?

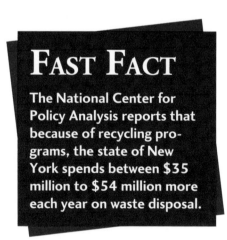

FAST FACT

The National Center for Policy Analysis reports that because of recycling programs, the state of New York spends between $35 million to $54 million more each year on waste disposal.

It was nine years ago that John Tierney's landmark article, entitled "Recycling Is Garbage" appeared in the *New York Times Magazine*. Focusing primarily on recycling efforts in New York City, he exposed the high expenses in collecting and separating the garbage, and the lack of demand for most of the resulting materials. Moreover, in some cases, such as recycling newspaper, more water pollution ensues (owing to removing the ink), than in making new paper. Besides, trees are specifically grown for this purpose, and are a renewable resource.

He also reassured the public on landfill site availability, noting that if Americans keep generating garbage at current rates for the next 1,000 years, and if all this refuse is put in a landfill 100 yards deep, by the year 3000, this accumulation of trash will fill a plot of land 35 miles on each side. This area, by the way, is about 5 percent the size of the space needed for solar panels, as touted by various environmental groups.

The Recycling Craze Began with a Fiasco

So, what's the big deal? Would it surprise you that the incident behind the hysteria over landfills, the infamous 1987 voyage of the barge *Mobro 4000*, containing 3,168 tons of Long Island trash, is a complete travesty? Chartered by entrepreneur Lowell Harrelson and

Samples of alternative lumber made from recycled sawdust and plastic.

A 2007 poll found that the majority of Americans recycle aluminum, paper, plastic, and glass without being forced by the government. Only about a fifth of the public said they recycle nothing at all.

Question: "In your own home, do you separate and recycle any of the following?"[x]	Total %	East %	Mid-West %	South %	West %
RECYCLE (NET)	77	88	70	68	86
Aluminum or metal cans	67	79	62	58	75
Paper	59	71	52	50	68
Plastic	57	74	51	46	65
Glass (bottles)	54	75	49	39	60
Cardboard	3	3	4	2	4
Batteries, motor oil, and other hazardous materials	2	3	2	*	2
Organic materials	2	1	*	*	5
Metal	1	1	1	1	1
Electronics	1	1	*	1	1
Something else	2	2	1	1	3
Nothing	23	12	30	32	14

x = Percentages may not add up to exactly 100% due to rounding.
* = less than 0.5%

Taken from: Harris Poll No. 67, "One-Quarter of Americans Do Not Recycle in Their Own Home," July 11, 2007.

Long Island mob boss Salvatore Avellino, the craft was headed for a pilot program in Morehead City, North Carolina to be turned into methane. But, before the barge reached its destination, a rumor began to circulate (never verified and most likely untrue) that the load contained medical waste. At that, the permits to unload were denied, and it continued to travel south, facing military force in Mexico, before finally arriving at a Brooklyn incinerator five months later.

Thus, given the bad publicity of mob ties and a vicious rumor, the recycling craze was born. Ironically, there never was a problem with finding a Long Island landfill. The whole thing occurred because Harrelson was trying to beat the high tipping fees of the local facilities, and assure himself of a big profit.

Tierney made many other strong points in his article, including a defense of Styrofoam coffee cups and the amount of waste at fast food restaurants. But, save a quick rebuttal from the Environmental Defense Fund (EDF), few voices were raised in opposition to his startlingly contrarian piece. As it was, the EDF essay contained numerous examples of classical fallacies in logic, and must have been embarrassing to even the group's most ardent supporters.

Voluntary Recycling Yields Useful Products

Are there any good news recycling stories? Certainly. Aluminum recycling is one of the original triumphs. Glass waste has been used in the production of new glass for decades. Engineered wood products, melding sawmill waste with newly harvested forest products, offer advantages over conventional goods in price, strength, and durability.

There is also an active market in plastics recycling. Poly-Wood, Inc. transforms milk jugs, once destined for landfills, into recycled plastic lumber used to create a pleasing line of casual outdoor furniture. For my money, it beats wicker and wood hands down. Recycline manufactures a range of personal care items, all from recycled plastic. The company also supplies postpaid mailers, for return of the products, into their destiny as plastic lumber.

Recycling Is Not Perfect and Should Not Be Mandatory

Plastic, far from being an environmental villain, as it has been portrayed, is proving itself to be highly recyclable, into products people actually want to buy. This should come as no surprise, since regrinding of plastic molding waste, for all applications except those that require clarity, is standard procedure. And, while paper is more biodegradable than plastic, this, too is a false issue, since in the low oxygen environment of landfills, neither paper nor plastic break down all that much. Another fad shattered?

Recycling surely has its place, and its role is growing, but it is not the holy grail. And, neither is technology the enemy, for without it, there would [be] scant time for environmental reason, or environmental reverie, for that matter.

EVALUATING THE AUTHOR'S ARGUMENTS:

In this viewpoint Michael D. Shaw uses history, facts, and examples to make his argument that the United States does not need recycling laws. He does not, however, use any quotations to support his point. If you were to rewrite this article and insert quotations, what authorities might you quote from? Where would you place these quotations to bolster the points Shaw makes?

The Government Should Lead Efforts to Recycle Electronics

"Without EPA authority to require recycling of these products ... these programs' successes have been and will continue to be limited."

U.S. Government Accountability Office

The following viewpoint was published by the U.S. Government Accountability Office, an agency that investigates how the federal government spends taxpayer dollars. The authors argue that in order to be effective, electronics recycling programs should be required and supported by the federal government. They explain why nongovernmental recycling programs do not work: Consumers have to pay a fee to recycle their electronics and are forced to drop them at inconvenient locations. Since electronics are not banned from landfills in forty-six states, many people instead choose to throw their electronics in landfills instead of recycling them (which the authors say is much better for the environment). However, programs that are sponsored by the federal government are highly successful. Only the government has the resources and manpower to make electronics recycling financially and environmentally feasible. Therefore, the authors conclude the government should strengthen its role as a leader in electronics recycling.

Electronic Waste: Strengthening the Role of the Federal Government in Encouraging Recycling and Reuse, Washington, DC: United States Government Accountability Office, 2005.

AS YOU READ, CONSIDER THE FOLLOWING QUESTIONS:
1. Out of 70 million computers, how many were recycled in 2003, according to the authors?
2. Out of thousands of federal agencies, how many participated in the Federal Electronics Challenge, say the authors?
3. What is Executive Order 12845 and what bearing does it have on the authors' argument?

R apid advances in technology have led to increasing sales of new electronic devices, particularly televisions, computers, and computer monitors. Approximately 62 percent of U.S. households had computers in 2003, compared with only 37 percent just 6 years earlier. With this increase comes the dilemma of how to manage these products when they reach the end of their useful lives. The National Safety Council forecast that in 2003 alone, about 70 million existing computers became obsolete, but it also forecast that only 7 million were recycled. . . .

Obstacles to Recycling

Despite the large volume of used electronics and the valuable resources contained within them, economic and regulatory factors discourage these products' recycling and reuse. Specifically:

- Consumers generally have to pay fees and drop off their used electronics at often inconvenient locations to have them recycled or refurbished for reuse. Consumers in Snohomish County, Washington, for instance, may have to travel more than an hour to the nearest drop-off location, which then charges between $10 and $27 per unit, depending on the type and size of the product. Consumers in the Portland, Oregon area pay one local recycler 50 cents per pound to have their used computers recycled, which is about $28 for an average-sized desktop computer. Recyclers and refurbishers charge these fees because costs associated with recycling and refurbishing outweigh the revenue received from recycled commodities or refurbished units. This point was underscored by the International Association of Electronics Recyclers, which reported that the value of commodities recovered from computer equipment (such as shredded plastic, copper, and aluminum) is only between $1.50 and $2.00 per unit. It was further underscored by our interviews with eight electronics recyclers, who were unanimous in emphasizing that they could not cover costs without charging fees.

• Federal regulatory requirements also provide little incentive for environmentally preferable management of used electronics. First, some used electronics are considered hazardous waste under RCRA [Resource Conservation and Recovery Act] and RCRA bars entities that generate more than 220 pounds per month of hazardous waste (including some used electronics) from depositing it in landfills. However, RCRA does not bar households and entities that generate less than 220 pounds of hazardous waste per month from this practice. Consequently, since only four states currently ban disposal of used electronics in landfills, most consumers in the remaining 46 states (and the District of Columbia)

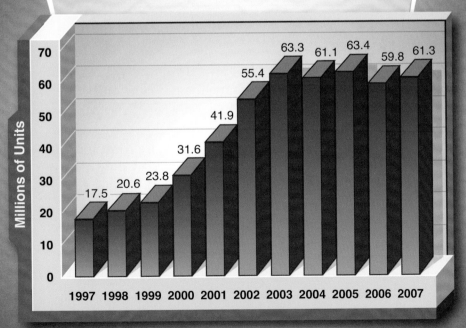

Estimated Number of Obsolete Home Computers

As more Americans use and retire computers, the amount of electronics waste is expected to grow.

Millions of Units

Year	Value
1997	17.5
1998	20.6
1999	23.8
2000	31.6
2001	41.9
2002	55.4
2003	63.3
2004	61.1
2005	63.4
2006	59.8
2007	61.3

Taken from: National Safety Council, Competitive Enterprise Institute.

are allowed to do so—and have little incentive to do otherwise. Not surprisingly, data we reviewed suggest that states and localities without landfill bans have dramatically lower levels of recycling than the four states that have enacted landfill bans. Second, federal law does not provide a financing system to recycle used electronics. Absent a consistent financing system to make recycling less costly and more convenient for consumers, a patchwork of potentially conflicting state requirements is emerging that may ultimately place a substantial burden on recyclers, retailers, and manufacturers. The lack of a national financing mechanism has also led to an array of legislative proposals that take very different approaches to address the problem. Third, federal regulations do not provide adequate oversight of these products when exported. This is a particular problem in the case of some developing countries, where risks to the environment and human health may be more likely because less stringent environmental regulations often do not ensure that exported used electronics—supposedly destined for reuse—are not instead being disposed of improperly. Together, these factors hinder EPA's [Environmental Protection Agency] ability to reach its stated goal that within 10 years, it will be as convenient for consumers to take a discarded television or computer for recycling or reuse as it is to purchase a new product.

Recycling Electronics Has Environmental and Financial Benefits

EPA has spent about $2 million on several voluntary programs to help overcome some of the factors discouraging recycling and reuse of used electronics. For example, the "Plug-In To eCycling" campaign sponsors partnerships with industry and state and local governments to make recycling used electronics less expensive and more convenient for consumers. In 2004, Plug-In To eCycling sponsored four pilot projects involving collection events at retailers such as Best Buy, Good Guys, Office Depot, and Staples, in which over 11 million pounds of used electronics were collected. Another program—the Federal Electronics Challenge—leverages U.S. government purchasing power to promote environmentally preferable management of used electronics throughout their life cycle: procurement, operation and maintenance, and end-of-life management. Through its participation in this program, the Bonneville

Power Administration [BPA] has already documented cost savings associated with longer life spans for the agency's computers and through purchases of computer monitors that contain less toxic substances and are therefore cheaper to recycle. To date, however, only 61 out of thousands of federal facilities participate in the Federal Electronics Challenge. A major reason for the limited federal participation in this and other EPA electronics recycling programs is that, unlike other successful federal procurement programs (such as EPA's and the Department of Energy's Energy Star program), participation is not required. . . .

Federal Laws Promote Recycling Participation

The Congress affirmed its commitment to reducing waste and encouraging recycling, first through enactment of the Resource Conservation and Recovery Act (RCRA) of 1976, and then again with passage of the Pollution Prevention Act of 1990. Both RCRA and the Pollution Prevention Act address alternatives to waste disposal. RCRA promotes the use of resource recovery, either through facilities that convert waste to energy or through recycling. To promote recycling, RCRA required EPA to develop guidelines for identifying products that are or can be produced with recovered materials. RCRA also required federal agencies to procure items that are, to the maximum extent practicable, produced with recovered materials. . . .

EPA has implemented several promising voluntary programs to encourage recycling and reuse of used electronics. Without EPA authority to require recycling of these products or to require other federal agencies to participate, however, these programs' successes have been and will continue to be limited. . . .

> **FAST FACT**
>
> The Consumer Electronics Association reports that 13.4 million computers were recycled in 2007, compared with 7.3 million in 2005.

Federal Agencies Set Higher Standards for Energy Efficient Products

Perhaps the best precedent for requiring broader federal participation in electronics recycling is the Energy Star program, co-sponsored by

Government electronics recycling programs include the Resource Conservation and Recovery Act. The Act bars companies with more than 220 pounds of hazardous waste from depositing it in landfills.

EPA and the Department of Energy. According to EPA, in 2004 alone, Energy Star products helped save approximately $10 billion in energy costs and reduced greenhouse gas emissions by an amount equivalent to that produced by 20 million automobiles. Also, in 2005, public awareness of Energy Star reached over 60 percent. Because of Energy Star's high profile, EPA officials told us that although manufacturers do not have to design their products to meet Energy Star criteria, many manufacturers view Energy Star as a de facto requirement for design of their products—suggesting that if their products do not have the Energy Star label then they are at a competitive disadvantage in the marketplace.

According to an EPA official who has worked on the Energy Star program since its inception, part of Energy Star's success can be attributed to two executive orders that required federal agencies to purchase products equipped with Energy Star features. Specifically, Executive Order 12845, issued in 1993, required federal agencies to procure computers and monitors that meet Energy Star requirements for energy efficiency. This EPA official told us that the early success of Energy Star was enhanced by this executive order. Executive Order 13123, issued in 1999, directs federal agencies to select Energy Star products when procuring *any* energy-using product. For product groups where Energy Star labels are not yet available, agencies are directed to select products that are in the upper 25 percent of energy efficiency, as designated by the Federal Energy Management Program.

Electronic Recycling Programs with No Federal Backing Have Limited Success

In contrast, the potential success of the FEC [Federal Electronics Challenge] and EPEAT [Electronic Product Environmental Assessment Tool] programs is presently limited because, unlike the Energy Star program, federal agencies' participation is not required. The potential benefits from broader federal participation were illustrated by BPA's experience, which, as noted earlier, demonstrated significant cost and energy savings and greater environmental protection. They were also underscored by the results of our survey—almost 90 percent of respondents said that federal government procurement criteria along the lines of FEC and EPEAT should be required, and over 95 percent said that such procurement criteria would encourage environmentally preferable product design, and greater recycling and reuse.

Despite the significant environmental benefits of recycling and reusing used electronics, these environmentally preferable practices will likely remain underutilized unless concerted actions are taken.

EVALUATING THE AUTHORS' ARGUMENTS:

The authors of this viewpoint, who represent a government agency, recommend that the federal government pass more laws to promote and assist used electronics recycling programs. Does knowing the source of the viewpoint influence your opinion of the recommendation made? Explain your answer thoroughly.

The Government Should Not Lead Efforts to Recycle Electronics

Dana Joel Gattuso

"Government fees, mandates, and regulations only create barriers to private efforts to find successful ways to recycle and reuse electronics."

In the following viewpoint author Dana Joel Gattuso argues that government regulations to recycle electronics are unnecessary, restrictive, and costly. She debunks myths about electronics recycling, claiming that electronic waste is not growing uncontrollably and computers in landfills do not contain toxic materials that endanger public health. Gattuso says it is therefore safe and less expensive to landfill more electronics waste rather than recycle it. Furthermore, for the electronics waste that should be recycled, Gattuso says that private companies have developed successful recycling methods that are efficient and make financial sense. Government recycling programs, on the other hand, are generally unsuccessful and do not generate enough revenue to cover costs, in Gattuso's opinion. For all these reasons, she concludes that private

Dana Joel Gattuso, *Mandated Recycling of Electronics: A Lose-Lose-Lose Proposition,* Washington, DC: Competitive Enterprise Institute, 2005. Reproduced by permission.

companies do the best job of recycling electronics, that most electronics waste should go to landfills, and that the government should get out of the recycling business.

Gattuso is a writer and policy analyst of environmental issues. She writes frequently for the Competitive Enterprise Institute, an environmental think tank based in Washington, DC, from which this viewpoint is taken.

AS YOU READ, CONSIDER THE FOLLOWING QUESTIONS:
1. According to the author, what percent of total municipal solid waste did e-waste constitute in 1999? In 2001?
2. According to Gattuso, how much does it cost to recycle one ton of e-waste vs. putting it in a landfill?
3. How many pounds of computers and computer equipment did Dell, HP, and IBM recycle in 2004, according to the author?

C oncern over the rapid growth of used computers and what to do with them once they expire has placed the issue of how best to handle electronic waste—or "e-waste"—at the forefront of waste policy at the federal, state, and local levels. Increasingly, propaganda fueled by politically driven environmental activists and a misinformed media is turning concern into hysteria. Fears are largely based on the following myths:

Myths About Recycling Electronics

Electronic waste is growing at a rapid and uncontrollable rate and is the fastest growing portion of the municipal waste stream. While the amount of e-waste has been increasing, it remains a tiny percent of the total municipal solid waste stream. According to the Environmental Protection Agency (EPA), e-waste—including discarded TVs, VCRs, DVD players, and audio systems, as well as personal computers, fax machines, and printers—constituted only 1 percent of the total municipal solid waste stream in 1999, the first year EPA calculated electronics discards. Data for 2001 again showed electronic devices had not increased as a percent of total municipal waste but remained at 1 percent.

Nor is e-waste growing at a rapid rate. National Safety Council (NSC) data show that the number of discarded computers will level off by 2005 at 63 million, and will then begin to decline. While improved technology can quickly make machines obsolete, it can also extend the lifespan of the next generation of computers. More powerful microchips will soon provide machines with much greater capacity.

Computers buried in landfills endanger public health because they contain toxic materials such as lead, cadmium, and mercury that can leak out into the soil and groundwater. Cathode ray tubes (CRTs), the most common type of computer display monitor, typically contain four pounds of lead to protect users from the tubes' x-rays, the same way a lead vest protects patients who have x-rays. Because lead is a health risk at high exposure levels, many lawmakers are rushing to ban display monitors and other electronics from municipal landfills, fearing that the lead and other toxic metals can leak out into the ground soil. . . .

It Is Safe to Throw Electronics in Landfills

Even if the natural conditions that prevent leaching did not occur, the sophisticated engineering and monitoring of today's modern municipal landfills, governed by stringent state and federal regulations and performance standards, prevents lead and other heavy metals from leaching. MSW [municipal solid waste] landfills are constructed with thick layers of clay and thick, puncture-resistant liners that keep waste from coming into contact with soil and groundwater. Also, landfills today are constructed with a leachate collection system—a system of pipes that carries any excess leachate out of the landfill and into a separate leachate collection pond where it is then tested and treated. In addition, landfills are surrounded by groundwater monitoring stations which capture samples of groundwater and continuously test for any possible leaks.

In summary, there is no scientific evidence that substances from e-waste present a discernable risk to human health or the environment when disposed of in municipal landfills. Yet widespread fear that lead and other metals in landfills can leach and present a health hazard has provoked lawmakers in a handful of states—California, Maine,

Electronics Recycling Is Not Necessary

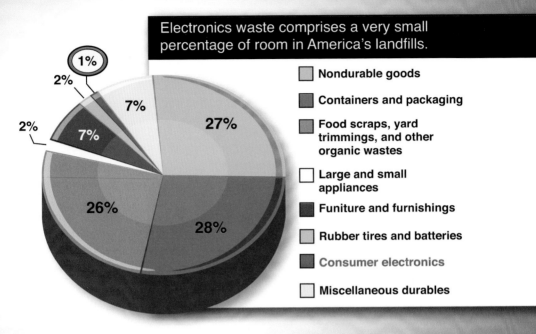

Electronics waste comprises a very small percentage of room in America's landfills.

- Nondurable goods
- Containers and packaging
- Food scraps, yard trimmings, and other organic wastes
- Large and small appliances
- Funiture and furnishings
- Rubber tires and batteries
- Consumer electronics
- Miscellaneous durables

Taken from: EPA, "Municipal Solid Waste in the United States: 2001 Facts and Figures," p. 70.

Massachusetts, and Minnesota—to ban desktop display monitors from landfills; another half a dozen have pending legislation.

Ironically, the problem is not so much electronic waste itself, but what to do with the enormous quantities of e-waste if lawmakers choose to ban it from landfills. Furthermore, lead and other compounds are considered by some experts to be safer when contained in landfills than during the recycling process when they become exposed. Finally, the cost difference is astronomical. Where a ton of e-waste can cost $500 to recycle, it costs only $40 to landfill. . . .

Mandatory Recycling Laws Are Problematic

The widely exaggerated and, in some cases, bogus assumptions concerning the dangers of used computers are creating widespread panic among policy makers who view the issue of e-waste as a desperate and uncontrollable situation. Moreover, these fears are driving perverse and harmful policy objectives in a frantic attempt to solve a non-existent crisis.

Policy makers, in the mistaken belief that recycling is the answer, increasingly are considering mandatory "take back" and/or recycling laws—that is, shifting the responsibility for waste back to the producer to recycle the waste—accompanied by "green design" mandates. Policy makers assume that requiring manufacturers to take back and recycle used products will create incentives for them to make more "eco-friendly" products.

Efforts in recycling e-waste at the federal, state, and local levels have been made more difficult due to environmental activists and a misinformed media, says the author.

This idea is an outgrowth of two concepts pushed by eco-activists: "product stewardship" and "extended producer responsibility." These policies hold that because natural resources are limited, measures must be taken to conserve those resources and that the best method is to hold the manufacturer responsible for the waste he produces. Further, it assumes the producer should be made to "internalize" environmental "external" costs so he will be motivated to minimize pollution, and that a pricing mechanism for the product will emerge that incorporates that universal cost. "Take-back" and mandated recycling laws are the direct result of the "producer responsibility" concept.

FAST FACT

The environmental group Basel Action Network has found that up to 80 percent of electronics that are collected for recycling are sent overseas, where workers are exposed to chemicals while extracting metal and glass from the products.

Recycling Laws Are Environmentally and Economically Risky

Most laws and regulations holding manufacturers responsible are not based on any real, identifiable environmental problem. Rather, they are a development of the "precautionary principle," a belief system also pushed by the environmental movement that holds if there is even a potential for an environmental risk, then measures must be taken to prevent that risk from ever occurring. One of the biggest problems with the "precautionary principle" is that it fails to consider tradeoffs—environmental, health, and economic.

Lawmakers throughout Europe and parts of Asia have widely adopted "extended producer responsibility" laws, particularly in an attempt to control waste from paper and packaging, tires, automobiles, batteries, some appliances, and, most recently, electronics. But studies analyzing the impact of these efforts show that these mandated recycling programs carry huge risks to both human health and the environment. Furthermore, consumers bear the burden of paying for these costly programs that compromise product quality and reliability by impeding innovation. . . .

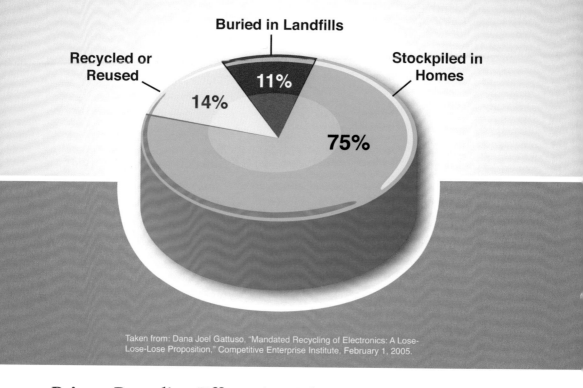

Where Are Obsolete Computers?

The majority of old computers are not being thrown away but stored in people's homes.

Buried in Landfills

Recycled or Reused

Stockpiled in Homes

11%

14%

75%

Taken from: Dana Joel Gattuso, "Mandated Recycling of Electronics: A Lose-Lose-Lose Proposition," Competitive Enterprise Institute, February 1, 2005.

Private Recycling Efforts Are Adequate

The nation's leading computer and electronics manufacturers, by running their own recycling programs for some time now, have developed skills beyond designing and constructing new computers: They now know how best and most effectively to take them apart. No two take-back and recycling programs are the same. Companies are testing and devising methods that best work for them, their contractors, and their customers.

Furthermore, because companies are in the driver's seat, they are continuously looking for ways to improve their recycling and reuse programs, making it easier for customers to return used products, and finding ways to collect and break down the used equipment more cost-effectively. As Dell Sustainable Business Director Pat Nathan told *The Dallas Morning News*, Dell is looking to "analyze data from suppliers and customers to develop more efficient recycling methods, eventually recycling computers at a lower cost than its competitors can and offering customers a lower price." Over time, these companies are learning how to cut costs. As a result, the collection fees that manufacturers charge consumers have remained constant or even declined—with some companies like Dell, Gateway, and HP providing customers with rebates for trading in used computers.

Government Recycling Efforts Cost Too Much

By contrast, local governments attempting to operate electronic collection and recycle services for residents are struggling, prompting states to enact fee programs to come to their rescue. But even the fees, which have risen on average by 40 to 100 percent since 2001, are failing to cover the costs.

Some argue that these recycling and reuse efforts by the private sector do not even come close to addressing the millions of obsolete electronics that are entering the waste stream each year. Yet this argument fails to acknowledge the enormous achievements the industry has made in a relatively short time. Last year [2004], Dell, HP, and IBM collectively recycled 160 million pounds of computers and computer equipment. This figure doesn't include the number of units remanufactured for donations and reuse.

Government Should Get Out of the Recycling Business

If the growing trend is for government to impose its own set of rules on how manufacturers should build and take apart electronics, producers and recyclers will be forced to abandon what works for them and follow a new set of rules. A burgeoning private marketplace of creative ideas and innovations, where producers compete to provide the best collection service at the lowest possible cost to the customer, will be replaced by a government bureaucracy that has no particular incentive—or ability—to keep costs down. . . .

Government—at the state and federal levels—should get out of the recycling business altogether. Government fees, mandates, and regulations only create barriers to private efforts to find successful ways to recycle and reuse electronics. Much of the waste can and is being handled by manufacturers, retailers, recyclers, and nonprofits, but these efforts will only succeed and grow if government gets out of the way. The remaining amount of waste can and should be placed in landfills designed, built, and regulated to handle hazardous waste far more toxic than that which is found in e-waste.

EVALUATING THE AUTHORS' ARGUMENTS:

In this viewpoint Gattuso argues that government-mandated electronics recycling limits innovation and drives up costs. How do you think the authors of the preceding viewpoint from the Government Accountability Office might respond to this argument? Explain your answer using evidence from the texts.

Viewpoint

5

City Governments Should Ban Plastic Bags

Jennifer Clapp

"Most of the local reasons given for reducing bag use have to do with their sheer volume and long-term persistence."

Local governments are justly banning the use of plastic bags because of environmental concerns, argues Jennifer Clapp in the following viewpoint. Clapp provides several examples of problems caused by plastic bags throughout the world, including clogged sewer drains, coastal and air pollution, and danger to marine and land animals. Plastic bag use has also caused many areas to become exceedingly dirty and even disease-ridden, she says. As a result, local governments around the globe have banned or severely restricted plastic bag use in an attempt to improve their local environments. Clapp applauds their efforts and encourages other communities to pass plastic bag bans.

Clapp is chair of Centre for International Governance Innovation, a leading international relations and policy research center at the University of Waterloo in Ontario, Canada. She also coedits the journal *Global Environmental Politics.*

Jennifer Clapp, "The Time Has Come to Kill All the Plastic Bags," *Globe and Mail* (Toronto), February 11, 2008. Reproduced by permission of the author.

AS YOU READ, CONSIDER THE FOLLOWING QUESTIONS:
  1. Name at least five countries in which local governments have banned plastic bags, according to the author.
  2. According to the author, how many years does it take for a plastic bag to break down?
  3. What does "white pollution" mean in the context of the viewpoint?

C hina is banning the distribution of free plastic shopping bags, effective this June. Australia says it will phase out plastic shopping bags by the end of 2008. These moves are just the latest in a string of official actions to restrict the use of plastic shopping bags.

Tanzania, Kenya, Uganda, major cities in India and Bangladesh and a growing number of towns in the United Kingdom have banned them. Ireland and South Africa have imposed steep taxes on them. And in North America, bans have been put in place in a number of cities, from San Francisco to Leaf Rapids, Man. [Manitoba, Canada].

Environmental Concerns Start at the Local Level

What explains this global movement against plastic shopping bags? Environmental concerns, of course.

Many assume that such rapid and widespread shifts in environmental policies around the world can only be the product of an international treaty or, at the very least, the outcome of a highly organized international campaign by leading environmental organizations. But, in the case of plastic bags, the movement appears to be largely local and largely ad hoc.

There is some debate over the environmental impact of plastic bags, particularly with respect to the amount of energy they embody when compared with other options. But the specific

FAST FACT

The U.S. Environmental Protection Agency estimates Americans use 380 billion plastic bags a year. Only 20 percent of paper bags and just 1 percent of plastic bags are recycled.

Plastic Bag Bans Around the World

Plastic bags have been banned or taxed in dozens of places around the globe.

United States

- **San Francisco:** Banned plastic bags in 2007.

Europe

- **United Kingdom:** Considering a ban on plastic bags.

- **Ireland:** Imposed a tax on plastic shopping bags in 2002.

- **Switzerland:** Shoppers pay extra to use a plastic bag.

- **Belgium:** Tax is levied on plastic bags.

- **Holland:** Surcharge for using plastic bags.

- **Germany:** Charges for plastic bags.

- **Italy:** Shoppers pay a tax if they use a plastic bag.

Asia

- **China:** Banned the use of thin (less than 0.1025 mm thick) plastic bags in January 2008.

- **Taiwan:** Taxes plastic bags.

- **Dhaka, Bangladesh, Mumbai:** Plastic bags are banned.

Africa

- **Eritrea:** Bans thin plastic bags.

- **Kenya:** Plastic bags are banned.

- **South Africa:** Banned thin plastic bags in 2003; thicker ones are taxed.

- **Uganda:** Plastic bag ban in effect.

- **Rwanda:** Thin plastic bags are banned.

Oceania

- **Australia:** Considering a ban on plastic bags.

The Chinese government has banned some types of plastic bags and charges customers a fee for the use of others. The Chinese were using 3 billion plastic bags a day. In some countries, reusable tote bags, like the one picture here, are used instead of plastic bags.

rationales for regulations against plastic bags often have been driven by very local concerns.

Plastic Bags Create Environmental Hazards

Most of the local reasons given for reducing bag use have to do with their sheer volume and long-term persistence. The Washington-based

Worldwatch Institute estimates that 500 billion plastic shopping bags are distributed and discarded every year, each of which can take up to 1,000 years to break down.

In India, discarded plastic bags on roadsides were being ingested by free-ranging cows, resulting in many deaths of the animals. In Dhaka, plastic bags were found to be the culprits in serious flooding by clogging sewer drains.

In Australia and Ireland, both countries that rely on the beauty of their coasts to attract tourists, there was a desire to present a clean image, as plastic bags were making up a significant amount of coastal litter. People there were also concerned about the dangers posed to marine life that can ingest, or get tangled in, plastic bags.

In a number of African countries, there are worries that plastic bags can act as breeding grounds for malaria-carrying mosquitoes. Plastic bags in China are known as "white pollution" because they are carelessly discarded in the streets.

San Francisco, in passing its ban, cited concern not just over litter and danger to sea mammals but also greenhouse-gas emissions associated with plastic bags, which are petroleum-based products. Leaf Rapids was worried about litter as well as the fact that household waste in thin plastic bags appeared to be attracting bears to its dump.

Local Laws Can Make a Global Impact

The global trend away from plastic bags has been bolstered by the fact that some retailers have been supportive. Some British retailers have backed voluntary bans, and several large chains in Canada and the United States have said they will stop handing out free plastic shopping bags altogether.

In many countries, the plastics industry prefers voluntary measures to control plastic bags through reuse and recycling, and opposes taxes and outright bans. Last year, Ontario and retail and industry groups voluntarily agreed to cut bag use by half over the next five years. The Ontario government noted that, if the voluntary measures are not successful, it will consider more stringent regulatory action.

The global shift in regulations vis-à-vis plastic bags demonstrates that rapid changes in governance practices around the world on environmental issues can take many forms, and can occur at many levels.

Internationally negotiated, top-down approaches may attract a lot of attention but don't always yield tangible results. Environmental initiatives that spring from the ground up and emerge from local concerns can collectively result in a powerful global impact, even without an internationally organized treaty or campaign.

EVALUATING THE AUTHOR'S ARGUMENTS:

In this viewpoint Jennifer Clapp uses the fact that increasing numbers of cities are banning plastic bags as a reason why more should do so. What do you think of this argument? Do you find it convincing? Why or why not?

Viewpoint

6

City Governments Should Not Ban Plastic Bags

Juliet S. Samuel

"Plastic bags are relatively harmless in environmental terms."

In the following viewpoint Juliet S. Samuel argues that local governments have poor reasons for banning plastic bags. Samuel contends that plastic bags are not as environmentally harmful as people believe. In Samuel's opinion, banning plastic bags will increase the use of paper bags, which discharge more pollutants, take more energy to produce and recycle, and take up more space in landfills than plastic. Furthermore, banning their use unfairly takes away consumer choice when shopping. She urges environmentalists and local policy makers to take a closer look at the long-term effects of banning plastic bags, arguing the bans are unnecessary and will create other environmental problems. Samuel warns the plastic bag ban craze will make consumers less likely to learn about what actually harms the environment and will halt progress on the continuous improvement of plastic bags.

Samuel writes regularly for the *Harvard Crimson*, the daily student newspaper of Harvard University.

AS YOU READ, CONSIDER THE FOLLOWING QUESTIONS:
 1. What percent of the total content of landfills are made up of plastic bags, as reported by the author?
 2. According to the author, how much less energy does it take to produce plastic bags compared with paper bags?
 3. Why does the author think the green, environmentally friendly image that appears on paper bags is misleading?

L ast month [March 2008], San Francisco's ban on the polyethylene plastic bag—cheap, convenient and 100 percent recyclable—celebrated its first anniversary (although it has only been in effect since September [2007]). The ban banished the bags from 50 of San Francisco's largest supermarkets and has reportedly reduced usage by five million bags so far. In its place: Government-mandated paper bags, compostable plastic, and reusable canvas sacks.

Plastic Bags Are Relatively Harmless

The ban on plastic bags was passed in March 2007 in order to stop consumers from making the wrong choice for the environment. But those responsible for the ban didn't seem to quite understand what that meant: "We're not taking away any choices," said Mark Westlund of the San Francisco Environmental Department. Pressed, he switched from denial to paternalism: "We've taken away a choice that is a detrimental choice."

And the trend has spread: At least 10 U.S. cities have considered or passed some form of ban on the innocent polyethylene bag, from Oakland to Boston, Annapolis to Portland. And, in an effort to seem green, government ministers from England to Australia have promised to wage war on plastic. Reportedly, plastic bags clog up landfills and kill fish; they guzzle oil and energy; they decay far slower than other waste and are difficult to recycle. In fact, the bans are a case of style over substance: Plastic bags are relatively harmless in environmental terms, and where they are a problem, the ultimate issue is littering, not bag use.

One problem is that those backing the bans seem to be confused as to the true impact of these flimsy sacks. Alderman Sam Shropshire, sponsor of a bill to ban them in Annapolis, Md., last year (the ban was rejected in November [2007]) compares plastic bag use to DDT: "It's wrong, it's immoral," he says, "They're inundating our environment."

Paper Bags Are Less Environmentally Friendly than Plastic Bags

Supposedly, littered bags wreak havoc on environmentally sensitive areas where they get caught in rivers and entangle birds and fish. But if the ban had gone through, the cure might have been worse than the disease: According to the EPA, paper bags discharge significantly more water and air pollutants than plastic.

Of course, plastic is derived from a non-renewable resource—oil. But it's misleading to claim that their use constitutes a crisis. All of America's annual 100 billion plastic bags are made from 12 million barrels of oil—0.15 percent of the U.S.'s total yearly oil consumption. And a Waste Characterization Study for California in 2004 concluded that the bags account for just 0.4 percent of the total content of landfills.

"NO PLASTIC BAGS, PLEASE. I DON'T WANT TO CONTRIBUTE TO GLOBAL WARMING!"

Yet some proponents of anti-plastic measures seem misinformed. "Any environmentalist would argue when push comes to shove, paper is better for the environment than plastic," says Maria Blanchard, Press Secretary to Massachusetts State Senator Brian Joyce, who wants to introduce a statewide tax on plastic bags in his home state. The senator's office needs to check its facts: According to ReusableBags.com, an organization founded to promote the use of canvas sacks, plastic bags take four times less energy to produce and 91 percent less energy to recycle than paper, and Professor Bill Rathje, director of The Garbage Project, says they are at least three times less voluminous, requiring fewer gas-guzzling trucks to move them around and taking up less space in landfills.

Banning Plastic Bags Takes Away Consumers' Choice

Of course, the idea is to encourage consumers to bring reusable canvas totes to the store instead of using paper—in Shropshire's case by mailing 15,000 of them to his constituents. But it's not the hemp bags' lack of availability that makes them unpopular—IKEA sells them for 59 cents. Consumers just aren't convinced that the personal and environmental benefits of using them are worth the inconvenience of carrying ten canvas sacks for the week's groceries. If they were, a ban wouldn't be necessary.

So the likely upshot of banning plastic is an increase in the use of paper bags, which cost more energy to produce and take up more space than plastic. Supposedly, paper is better anyway, because it has a higher recycling rate than plastic—around 20 percent versus a rather dismal one percent. But the comparison is not entirely apt: The country currently uses only 7 billion paper sacks per year, compared to 100 billion plastic bags. And paper has an organic, green image, making its uses more likely to be the recycling type. When the average consumer, no more or less

> **FAST FACT**
>
> According to the Reason Foundation, it takes the energy equivalent of 8,300 barrels of oil to manufacture 100 million plastic bags, compared with the equivalent of 15,100 barrels to make the same number of paper bags.

An environmental technician sorts through paper and biodegradable plastic bags in a landfill so that their biodegradable characteristics can be compared.

informed than she was yesterday, finds her most convenient shopping option banned she's unlikely to start recycling soggy paper sacks.

Plastic Bag Ban Stops Progress

And most importantly, a ban is the one sure way to stop progress in its tracks. Modern plastic bags are the most environmentally friendly yet: They thinned down a third between 1977 and 1990, and have even started to appear in biodegradable form (at least these compostable bags are exempt from the San Francisco ban). Banning the product removes the incentive to improve it, just as it discourages individuals from educating themselves about their choices. Environmentalists need to reflect upon these long-term consequences before they charge in with sledgehammers to kill flies. Their current mentality—"for your own good"—simply isn't sustainable.

EVALUATING THE AUTHOR'S ARGUMENTS:

Samuel suggests that if plastic bags were really that bad for the environment, a ban on them would not be necessary—consumers would opt out of using them on their own. What do you think of this argument? Do you agree, or do you think her reasoning is flawed? Explain your answer using evidence from the texts you have read.

Facts About Garbage and Recycling

Editor's note: These facts can be used in reports or papers to reinforce or add credibility when making important points or claims.

Garbage

- According to the organization Health Care Without Harm, the average American throws away six hundred times his or her adult weight in garbage every year. This adds up to more than ninety thousand pounds of garbage over a lifetime.
- The organization Earth 911 reports that 80 percent of plastic water bottles wind up in landfills.
- According to Inform Inc., the average garbage truck gets less than three miles per gallon of gas. U.S. garbage trucks use 1 billion gallons of diesel fuel each year.
- According to the UN Environment Programme, plastic debris is the cause of death for more than 1 million seabirds each year.
- According to the Marine Conservation Society, adults use an average of three hundred plastic bags each year.
- The International Association of Electronics Recyclers reports that 400 million units of consumer electronic equipment are discarded each year.

According to the Electronics TakeBack Coalition:

- Americans generated 2.6 million tons of electronic waste in 2005, of which only 12.6 percent was recycled.
- 133,000 personal computers are thrown out in the United States each day.

According to the National Safety Council, as many as 680 million computers will become obsolete within the next few years, and this waste will contain more than 4 billion pounds of plastic and 1 billion pounds of lead.

The Environmental Protection Agency reports that consumer electronics make up 2 percent of the municipal solid waste stream.

According to Greenpeace, thirty-one species of marine mammals have been reported to have ingested marine debris.

A study by the United Nations found that manufacturing a computer and monitor requires 530 pounds of fossil fuel and 1.5 tons of water.

About one-third of an average dump is made up of packaging material.

Every year, each American sends about twelve hundred pounds of organic garbage that can be composted to landfills.

According to the Competitive Enterprise Institute, it costs about $500 to recycle a ton of electronics waste but only about $40 to put it in a landfill.

According to the National Parks Service, it takes:
- 1 million years for a glass bottle to decompose
- 600 years for fishing line to decompose
- 450 years for a plastic bottle to decompose
- 450 years for disposable diapers to decompose
- 200 years for an aluminum can to decompose
- 50 years for leather to decompose
- 50 years for a plastic cup to decompose
- 2 years for a cigarette butt to decompose
- 3 months for a waxed milk carton to decompose
- 2 months for an apple core to decompose
- 6 weeks for newspaper to decompose

Recycling
On average, it costs $30 per ton to recycle trash, $50 to send it to the landfill, and $65 to $75 to incinerate it.

According to the Environmental Protection Agency:
- 5 percent of glass containers are recycled
- 42 percent of the paper thrown away in the United States is recycled
- 40 percent of plastic soft drink bottles are recycled
- 55 percent of aluminum soft drink and beer cans are recycled
- 57 percent of steel packaging is recycled

- 52 percent of all major appliances are recycled
- 88 percent of newspapers are recycled.

According to beverage industry consultant R.W. Beck, Inc.:
- 40 million plastic bottles—most of them from bottled water—are thrown in the trash or tossed as litter every day.
- Only 12 percent of plastic bottles from water, juice, and sports beverages are recycled, compared with 30 percent of soft drink bottles.

The Environmental Protection Agency reports that Americans recycled 82 million tons of material in 2006 out of the 251 million tons of trash they generated.

According to the Container Recycling Institute:
- The rate of aluminum can recycling declined from 65 percent in 1992 to 45 percent in 2005.
- Only 33.5 percent of beverage containers were recycled in 2004, 20 percentage points lower than in 1992.
- Only 33.5 percent of beverage containers are recycled.

According to a survey by the Consumer Electronics Association, 63 percent of respondents said that recycling was very important.

According to Alcoa (Aluminum Company of America), 105,784 cans are recycled each minute.

The eleven states with "bottle bills" have recycling rates of 70 percent and higher, according to the Container Recycling Institute.

According to the Consumer Electronics Association, the number of recycled consumer electronic units increased by 26 percent from 2005 to 2007 (70.7 million units to 55.9 million units).

The Results of Recycling
According to the National Recycling Coalition, the Environmental Protection Agency, and Earth911.org:
- A used aluminum can is recycled and back on the grocery shelf as a new can in as little as sixty days.

- Used aluminum beverage cans are the most recycled item in the United States, but other types of aluminum, such as siding, gutters, car components, storm window frames, and lawn furniture can also be recycled.
- Recycling one aluminum can saves enough energy to run a TV for three hours, which is the equivalent of half a gallon of gasoline.
- There is no limit to the amount of times an aluminum can can be recycled.
- Recycling a single run of the Sunday *New York Times* would save seventy-five thousand trees.
- The average American uses seven trees a year in paper, wood, and other products made from trees. This amounts to about 2 billion trees per year.
- The amount of wood and paper thrown away each year is enough to heat 50 million homes for twenty years.
- Americans use 85 million tons of paper a year; about 680 pounds per person.
- The average household throws away thirteen thousand separate pieces of paper each year. Most is packaging and junk mail.
- Americans use 2.5 million plastic bottles every hour.
- American throw away 25 billion Styrofoam coffee cups every year.
- The energy saved from recycling one glass bottle can run a 100-watt lightbulb for four hours. It also causes 20 percent less air pollution and 50 percent less water pollution than making a new bottle from raw materials.

According to the organization Recycling International, producing paper from recycled paper creates 35 percent less water pollution than paper made from pulp.

According to the organization Health Care Without Harm, with the amount of energy it takes to make one new aluminum can, twenty cans can be made from recycled aluminum.

According to Alcoa:
- Recycling keeps 1.7 billion pounds of trash out of landfills.
- Recycling aluminum cans uses 95 percent less energy than making the cans from virgin ore.
- Americans earn approximately $1 billion annually by recycling aluminum cans.

- The energy saved by recovering a pound of aluminum can generate 7.5 kilowatt-hours of electricity, according to Alcoa.

According to the environmental organization I Love a Clean San Diego (ILACSD), if each American recycled one newspaper per week, 36 million trees would be saved each year.

The U.S. Department of Energy reports that recycling and composting divert more than 70 million tons of material from landfills.

Recycling supports 1.1 million American jobs, according to the National Recycling Coalition.

According to the Stanford Recycling Center:
- Each ton of PET plastic containers made from recycled plastic saves 7,200 kilowatt-hours.
- One ton of recycled aluminum saves forty barrels of oil.

The Steel Recycling Institute reports that the amount of energy saved by recycling steel can electrically power the equivalent of 18 million homes for a year.

According to the U.S. Recycling Economic Information Study, businesses that specialize in recycling and reusing earn $236 billion in gross revenues each year.

According to the EPA:
- The amount of recycling that occurred in 2005 saved 900 trillion British thermal units (Btu), or the amount of energy used by 9 million households in one year.
- The energy saved by recycling 1 million cell phones can provide more than nineteen thousand American households with one year's worth of electricity.

The Pennsylvania Department of Environmental Protection states that recycling reduces greenhouse gas emissions by 2 million metric tons of carbon.

According to the Newspaper Association of America, approximately 31 percent of recycled newspaper is turned into new newsprint.

Organizations to Contact

The editors have compiled the following list of organizations concerned with the issues debated in this book. The descriptions are derived from materials provided by the organizations. All have publications or information available for interested readers. The list was compiled on the date of publication of the present volume; the information provided here may change. Be aware that many organizations take several weeks or longer to respond to inquiries, so allow as much time as possible.

Bluewater Network
311 California St., Ste. 510, San Francisco, CA 94104
(415) 544-0790
e-mail: bluewater@bluewaternetwork.org
Web site: www.bluewaternetwork.org

The Bluewater Network promotes policy changes in government and industry to reduce dependence on fossil fuels and eradicate other root causes of air and water pollution, global warming, and habitat destruction. On its Web site the Bluewater Network publishes fact sheets on specific water pollution issues such as ship emissions, oil spills, and global warming. Articles that are available on the Web site include "Banishing Snowmobiles," "Super-Sized Cruise Ships Leave Wake of Wastes," and "Dirty Diesels."

Coalition for Responsible Waste Incineration (CRWI)
1615 L St. NW, Ste. 1350, Washington, DC 20036
(202) 452-1241
e-mail: mel@crwi.org
Web site: www.crwi.org

The coalition is made up of twenty-eight companies that are interested in hazardous waste combustion. The goal of CRWI is to reduce hazardous industrial waste and work with legislators to develop environmentally sound laws on hazardous waste management. The coalition publishes a monthly newsletter.

Container Recycling Institute (CRI)
89 E. Lake Shore Trail, Glastonbury, CT 06033
(202) 263-0999
Web site: www.container-recycling.org

CRI studies and promotes policies and programs that increase recovery and recycling of beverage containers and shift the social and environmental costs associated with manufacturing, recycling, and disposal of container and packaging waste from government and taxpayers to producers and consumers. CRI plays a vital role in educating policy makers, government officials, and the general public regarding the social and environmental impacts of the production and disposal of no-deposit, no-return beverage containers and the need for producers to take responsibility for their wasteful packaging.

Earth Island Institute (EII)
300 Broadway, Ste. 28, San Francisco, CA 94133-3312
(415) 788-3666
Web site: www.earthisland.org

Founded in 1982 by veteran environmentalist David Brower, EII develops and supports projects that counteract threats to the biological and cultural diversity that sustain the environment. Through education and activism, EII promotes the conservation, preservation, and restoration of Earth. EII publishes the quarterly *Earth Island Journal.* Recent articles are available on the EII Web site, including "Breathless in Harlem," "Toxic Toast and Radioactive Raisin Bran," and "Cruise Ships Fail Pollution Tests."

Environmental Defense Fund (EDF)
257 Park Ave. South, New York, NY 10010
(212) 505-2100
Web site: www.edf.org

The fund is a nonprofit organization of lawyers, scientists, and economists that works to develop innovative and cost-effective answers to environmental problems. Publications by EDF include "FAQs: Environmental Benefits of Recycled Paper" and "Buy Recycled . . . and Save."

Environment Canada

70 Crémazie St., Gatineau, QC K1A 0H3, Canada

(819) 997-2800

e-mail: enviroinfo@ec.gc.ca

Web site: www.ec.gc.ca

Environment Canada is a department of the Canadian government whose goal is to achieve sustainable development in Canada through environmental protection and conservation. Information about recycling is available on the Web site.

GrassRoots Recycling Network (GRRN)

4200 Park Blvd., #290, Oakland, CA 94602

(510) 531-5523

Web site: www.grrn.org

GRRN's mission is to eliminate the waste of natural and human resources. The network advocates corporate accountability and public policies that eliminate waste and build sustainable communities. The GRRN Web site includes fact sheets, reports, and articles, including "Composting and Organics: Recycling vs. Bioreactors" and "Beyond Recycling: The Zero Waste Solution."

Greenpeace USA

702 H St. NW, Washington, DC 20001

(202) 462-1177

e-mail: info@wdc.greenpeace.org

Web site: www.greenpeace.org

Greenpeace is an international environmental organization that aims to protect the oceans and promote a future free of toxic waste. Its publications include *Guide to Greener Electronics* and "Where Does E-Waste Go?"

INFORM

5 Hanover Sq., Flr. 19, New York, NY 10004-2638

(212) 361-2400

Web site: www.informinc.org

INFORM is an organization that looks for innovative practices and technologies to address environmental problems. Reports and fact sheets are available on the Web site, including "The Benefits of Recycling Electronics in the US" and "Greening Garbage Trucks: New Technologies for Cleaner Air."

National Recycling Coalition (NRC)
805 Fifteenth St. NW, Ste. 425, Washington, DC 20005
(202) 789-1430
e-mail: info@nrc-recycle.org
Web site: www.nrc-recycle.org

NRC is a nonprofit organization that aims to advance and improve recycling, reuse, and waste prevention. It seeks to encourage recycling efforts through changes in national policies on energy, waste management, taxes, and transportation. It publishes the e-newsletter *Mobius*.

National Solid Wastes Management Association (NSWMA)
4301 Connecticut Ave. NW, Ste. 300, Washington, DC 20008
(202) 244-4700
e-mail: membership@envasns.org
Web site: www.nswma.org

NSWMA is a trade association that represents for-profit companies that provide waste collection, recycling, and disposal services. Its goal is to promote environmentally responsible and ethical waste management. Publications on the Web site include *Research Bulletins*, "Profiles in Garbage" fact sheets, and the monthly magazine *Waste Age*.

Natural Resources Defense Council (NRDC)
40 W. Twentieth St., New York, NY 10011
(212) 727-2700
e-mail: nrdcinfo@nrdc.org
Web site: www.nrdc.org

The council is an environmental group of lawyers and scientists who help write environmental laws and seek to protect the quality of land, air, and water. The NRDC conducts research into topics such as cleaning up the oceans and removing toxic chemicals from the environment. NRDC publishes the quarterly magazine *OnEarth*, a monthly e-mail newsletter, and reports on environmental issues, including *Testing the Waters 2008: A Guide to Water Quality at Vacation Beaches.*

Political Economy Research Center (PERC)
2048 Analysis Dr., Ste. A, Bozeman, MT 59718
(406) 587-9591
e-mail: perc@perc.org
Web site: www.perc.org

PERC is a research and education foundation that focuses primarily on environmental and natural resource issues. It emphasizes the advantages of free markets and the importance of private property rights regarding environmental protection. Publications include "Eight Great Myths of Recycling." Other articles about garbage and recycling are on the Web site.

Sierra Club
85 Second St., 2nd Flr., San Francisco, CA 94105
(415) 977-5500
e-mail: information@sierraclub.org
Web site: www.sierraclub.org

Founded in 1892, Sierra Club is the oldest grassroots environmental organization in the United States. Its Zero Waste Committee aims to lead the nation in a transition from traditional waste disposal programs to comprehensive recycling systems. The organization publishes *Sierra* magazine six times a year.

UN Environment Programme (UNEP)
900 Seventeenth St. NW, Ste. 506, Washington, DC 20006
(202) 785-0465
Web site: www.unep.org

The goal of the UNEP is to help nations and their citizens improve their quality of life while caring for the environment. Reports on recycling are available on the Web site, and the organization publishes the magazine *Our Planet* three times a year.

U.S. Environmental Protection Agency (EPA)
1200 Pennsylvania Ave. NW, Washington, DC 20460
(202) 272-0167
Web site: www.epa.gov

The EPA is the government agency charged with protecting human health and safeguarding the natural environment. It works to protect Americans from environmental health risks, enforce federal environmental regulations, and ensure that environmental protection is an integral consideration in U.S. policy. The EPA publishes many reports, fact sheets, and educational materials, including "Electronics: A New Opportunity for Waste Prevention, Reuse, and Recycling" and *Consumer's Handbook for Reducing Solid Waste.*

For Further Reading

Books

Burns, Loree Griffin. *Tracking Trash: Flotsam, Jetsam, and the Science of Ocean Motion*. Boston: Houghton Mifflin, 2007. Explains what happens to trash that ends up in the ocean.

Girling, Richard. *Rubbish! Dirt on Our Hands and the Crisis Ahead*. London: Transworld, 2005. Explores the history of trash, particularly in England, and evaluates different solutions to the problems of waste.

Love, Ann, and Jan Drake. *Trash Action: A Fresh Look at Garbage*. Plattsburgh, NY: Tundra Books of Northern New York, 2006. Offers ways for people to reduce their consumption and become less wasteful.

Melosi, Martin V. *Garbage in the Cities: Refuse Reform and the Environment*. Pittsburgh: University of Pittsburgh Press, 2004. Explains how waste management has developed since the Progressive Era.

Pichtel, John. *Waste Management Practices: Municipal, Hazardous, and Industrial*. Boca Raton, FL: Taylor and Francis, 2005. Offers an overview of the development of waste management and the different technologies that are used to dispose of solid and hazardous wastes.

Rogers, Heather. *Gone Tomorrow: The Hidden Life of Garbage*. New York: New Press, 2006. Explores the history of waste disposal and how waste moves to landfills or incinerators. Also examines the flaws of recycling.

Royte, Elizabeth. *Garbage Land: On the Secret Trail of Trash*. Boston: Back Bay, 2006. Investigates the waste disposal process in the United States.

Schlesinger, Mark E. *Aluminum Recycling*. Boca Raton, FL: CRC, 2006. Details the process of aluminum recycling and looks at its economics and environmental challenges.

Scott, Nicky. *Reduce, Reuse, Recycle: An Easy Household Guide*. White River Junction, VT: Chelsea Green, 2007. Addresses a variety of common recycling questions, such as how to recycle cell phones and motor oil.

Yarrow, Joanna. *How to Reduce Your Carbon Footprint: 365 Simple Ways to Save Energy, Resources, and Money.* San Francisco: Chronicle, 2008. Details five hundred ways to conserve energy and prevent pollution, including recycling.

Zimring, Carl A. *Cash for Your Trash: Scrap Recycling in America.* Piscataway, NJ: Rutgers University Press, 2005. Details the history of scrap recycling in the United States.

Periodicals

Allsopp, Michelle, Adam Walters, David Santillo, and Paul Johnston, "Plastic Debris in the World's Oceans," Greenpeace International, 2006. www.unep.org/regionalseas/marinelitter/publications/docs/plastic_ocean_report.pdf.

Bailey, Ronald. "Happy Birthday, Love Canal," *Reason*, March 24, 2004.

Clark, Maggie. "Making Zero Waste Part of the Plan," *Gotham Gazette*, April 21, 2008. www.gothamgazette.com/article/sustainability watch/20080421/210/2500.

Clayton, Mark. "Congress Acts to Clean Up the Ocean," *Christian Science Monitor*, October 11, 2006.

Cohen, Steve. "Wasted: New York City's Giant Garbage Problem," *New York Observer*, April 3, 2008.

Cooper, Sean. "Houston, We Have a Trash Problem," *Wired*, May 2007.

Davis, Sheila. Testimony to the Senate Subcommittee on Superfund and Waste Management, Environment and Public Works Committee, July 26, 2005. www.epw.senate.gov/109th/Davis_testimony.pdf.

Dennen, Sally. "How to Recycle Practically Everything," *E: The Environmental Magazine*, May/June 2006.

Dumke, Mike. "The Plastic Plague," *Chicago Reader*, March 6, 2008.

Economist, "The Truth About Recycling," June 7, 2007. www.economist.com/search/displaystory.cfm?story_id=9249262.

Franklin, Matthew. "Scientists Trash Plastic Bag Ban," *Australian*, August 19, 2008.

Gattuso, Dana Joel. "Mandated Recycling of Electronics: Creating a Mountain Out of a Landfill," *Monthly Planet*, April 30, 2005.

Kalkowski, John. "To Boost Recycling, Make It Profitable," *Converting Magazine*, January 1, 2008.

Kiernan, Ian. "The Toxic Legacy of Plastic Bags," *Australian Broadcasting Company*, January 26, 2008. www.abc.net.au/news/stories/2008/01/25/2146339.htm.

Lehr, Jay. "Recycling: Your Time Can Be Better Spent!" *Heartland Institute*, April 1, 2003. www.heartland.org/Article.cfm?artId=11735.

Lopez, Steve. "We Will Be Known by the Junk We Throw Away," *Los Angeles Times*, September 12, 2007.

Lowy, Joan. "Plastic Left Holding the Bag as Environmental Plague," *Seattle Post-Intelligencer*, July 21, 2004.

Lush, Tamara. "Ban Those Bags," *Miami New Times*, October 11, 2007.

Marks, Kathy, and Daniel Howden, "The World's Rubbish Dump: A Garbage Tip That Stretches from Hawaii to Japan," *Independent* (London), February 5, 2008. www.independent.co.uk/environment/the-worlds-rubbish-dump-a-garbage-tip-that-stretches-from-hawaii-to-japan-778016.html.

Moore, Charles. "Across the Pacific Ocean, Plastics, Plastics, Everywhere," *Natural History*, vol. 112, no. 9, November 2003.

———. "Out in the Pacific Plastic Is Getting Drastic," Agalita.org. http://marine-litter.gpa.unep.org/documents/World's_largest_landfill.pdf.

Torres, Nichole L. "Tech Recycling," *Entrepreneur*, December 2005.

Toto, DeAnne. "Renewing Curbside Recycling," *Recycling Today*, December 2006.

Weiss, Kenneth R. "Plague of Plastic Chokes the Seas," *Los Angeles Times*, August 2, 2006.

Wente, Margaret. "A Waste of Time and Money," *Reader's Digest*, January 2006.

Woods, Amanda. "The Plastic Killing Fields," *Sydney Morning Herald* (Sydney, Australia), December 29, 2007.

Zaleski, Olivia. "China's Plastic Bag Ban Will Save 37 Million Barrels of Oil: China Leapfrogs Other Nations with Simple Message: Bring Your Own Bag," *Daily Green.com*, January 9, 2008. www.thedailygreen.com/environmental-news/latest/china-plastic-bags-47010907.

Web Sites

Earth 911 (www.earth911.org). Earth 911 provides information on recycling in order to help consumers live responsibly and contribute to a sustainable environment. Information on recycling and composting and a monthly newsletter are available on the site.

Global Recycling Network (www.grn.com). This site provides news on recycling and information on environmentally friendly products.

Recycling Revolution (www.recycling-revolution.com). Contains a wealth of information about recycling and recycling programs.

Reduce, Reuse, Recycle (www.epa.gov/epawaste/conserve/rrr/index.htm). This page on the Environmental Protection Agency Web site provides facts about garbage and recycling and explains how people can reduce the amount of waste they create.

Reducing Unwanted Mail (www.epa.gov/osw/wycd/catbook/mail.htm). This page instructs Americans on how to reduce the number of catalogues, credit card offers, circulars, and other junk mail they receive.

Reusable Bags.com (www.reusablebags.com). This site contains information on ways people can reduce their use of disposable plastic and paper bags.

Index

Dhaka, 121, 123

San Francisco
recycling in, 40–41, 68
restrictions on plastic bags in,
39–40, 46, 123, 126
Sandwich bale, 69
Santillo, David, 33–34
Sea birds, threat of garbage to,
27–30
Sea lions, 28
Seals, 28
Sewage-related debris, 26
Shaw, Michael D., 97
Sheehan, Bill, 57
Ships, wastes from, 26
Single-stream collection, 66–68
South Africa, 120, 121
Spain, 93
Spectroscopic separator, *54*
Steel, 69, 82
Steele, Sally, 95
Sustainable Packaging Coalition,
69
Sweden, recycling in, 59–63
Switzerland, 121

T
Taiwan, 121
Tantalum, 81
Tanzania, 120
Throwaway society, 13–*14*
Tierney, John, 98–99, 101
Tourism, 26
Toxic chemicals, 13
Transportation, of garbage, 73–74,
89
Trash. *See* Garbage
Trees, 43, 80, 98

Trex, 42
Turtles, 28

U
Uganda, 120, 121
United Kingdom. *See* Britain
United Nations Environment
Programme, 7
United States
beverage container recycling in,
62
lack of space for garbage disposal
in, 12–17
recycling in, 55, 57, 65, 93, 100
recycling infrastructures in, 55
as throwaway society, 13–*14*
U.S. Government Accountability
Office, 103

V
Voluntary recycling, 101

W
Wal-Mart, 69
Waldman, Daniel, 17
Waste & Resources Action
Programme (WRAP), 65–66
Waste Management, 14
Water pollution, 83
Westlund, Mark, 42, 126
Whales, 28
Wildlife. *See* Marine animals
Wiseman, A. Clark, 21

Z
Zeller, Tom, Jr., 52
Zero-waste targets, 70

Picture Credits

Maury Aaseng, 16, 20, 29, 54, 62, 67, 76, 81, 88, 93, 100, 105, 113, 116, 121

© age fotostock/SuperStock, 11, 14, 22, 56, 87

© Ambient Images Inc./Alamy, 8

AP Images, 90, 95, 114

Romain Blanquart/MCT/Landov, 108

© Copyright 2007 Bob Englehart, *The Hartford Courant* and PoliticalCartoons.com, 127

Courtesy of NaturalNews.com, 48

Image copyright Tonis Valing, 2008. Used under license from Shutterstock.com, 34

© Katharine Andriotis Photography, LLC/Alamy, 39

James Keyser/Time Life Pictures/Getty Images, 99

Peter Macdiarmid/Getty Images, 82

© Rick Maiman/Sygma/Corbis, 75

© Mike Nelson/epa/Corbis, 27

© Qrt/Alamy, 61

© Roger Ressmeyer/Corbis, 129

© Jean Schweitzer/Alamy, 68

David Silverman/Getty Images, 51

© Dan Sullivan/Alamy, 47

© Pat Tuson/Alamy, 122